The HANGING of LUCKY BILL

WITHDRAWN

by
Michael J. Makley

Eastern Sierra Press
16 Pioneer Trail
Woodfords, California 96120
(916) 694-2711

The Hanging of Lucky Bill
  by Michael J. Makley

Published by:

Eastern Sierra Press
16 Pioneer Trail
Woodfords, California 96120
(916) 694-2711

Cover by Dorothy Makley.

Back cover photo, "Lucky Bill's coffin," courtesy of The Nevada Historical Society.

Copyright 1993 Michael J. Makley

All rights reserved. No part of this book may be reproduced or transmitted in any form or by any means, electronic or mechanical; including photocopying, recording or by any other information or retrieval system without written permission from the author, except for the inclusion of brief quotations in a review.

Library of Congress Catalogue Number 93-90318

ISBN: 0-9636608-0-2

Printed in the United States of America

ACKNOWLEDGMENTS

Thank you to Dorothy Makley for the art; F.J. Makley for suggestions about the manuscript; Dan Makley and Coach Mike Rippee for reading and commenting on early versions of the book; George Williams III for invaluable advice and editorial direction; Lennie Schwartz for computer expertise and design; David Thompson and Jeff Corzine for information on early Nevada; Dan Jones for artistic concepts; Jan Louch and the staff at Douglas County Library for assistance with the Van Sickle Collection; Eric Moody for locating maps; Mary Wood at Alpine County Library for locating out of print titles; the staffs at the California Section of California State Library, Nevada State Archives, The Sacramento County Library and The Nevada Historical Society for professional assistance; Kevin Makley for research at Livingston's Exchange; and Randi Lee for insight and support from the book's inception to completion.

Table of Contents

ACKNOWLEDGMENTS
INTRODUCTION 7
EXTRACTS 10

Chapter One	CARSON VALLEY	17
Chapter Two	1854 AND 1855	24
Chapter Three	MORMONS AND INDIANS	32
Chapter Four	MAJOR ORMSBY	41
Chapter Five	THE COLLAPSE OF GOVERNMENT	47
Chapter Six	A DESPERATE FIGHT	51
Chapter Seven	PRINCIPALS	55
Chapter Eight	MORALS AND MURDER	64
Chapter Nine	THE VIGILANTES ACT	89
Chapter Ten	THE ARRESTS AND TRIAL	95
Chapter Eleven	THE EXECUTION	105
Chapter Twelve	FATES OF THE PRINCIPALS	108

NOTES 118
BIBLIOGRAPHY 131
INDEX 135

Woodfords Canyon, through which Lucky Bill constructed his toll road.

Introduction

by George Williams III

Lucky Bill Thorington was a notorious character in northwestern Nevada Territory in the 1850's. In one of the most wicked places in the American West, amongst an assortment of crooks, liars, murderers and horse thieves, Thorington had sufficient decency to stand out like a beacon. Lucky Bill was a gambler; he was also a good businessman; he ran a hotel, ranch and toll road and provided various supplies to emigrants passing through Carson Valley on their way across the Sierra Nevada Mountains to Placerville, California. He was married, albeit to two women, and he had a son. He was a family man. Thorington had helped many a lonesome and sorry traveler who passed his way. Amongst his neighbors and those who knew him well, Lucky Bill Thorington had a good reputation. Certainly far better than some of the men who hanged him.

Lucky Bill apparently earned his name "Lucky" by being very adept at a primitive early Nevada gambling game called thimblerig. In fact, he was so good at this game, that he always warned his future victim that they would likely lose their shirts if they played against him. Ah, but the Pride of Man. Lucky Bill's victims always ignored his advice. And they were always beaten. Afterward, Bill's victims, poorer for the wear and tear, said bad things about Lucky Bill.

But certainly, being technically proficient at a primitive gambling game is no reason to hang a man. And that is what happened to Lucky Bill.

8   The Hanging of Lucky Bill

Author Michael Makley grew up in the Sierra Nevada Mountains not far from where Lucky Bill was murdered. Makley stumbled across Thorington's tragedy, and after reading through what little material he could find about Thorington's hanging, decided to look for more. What disturbed Makley most was to learn that Thorington's enemies were busy building a gallows even before the jury had reached a verdict. It must be a real lonesome feeling for a man to sit before a jury of his enemies for a murder he did not commit, to hear just beyond the opened window, the pounding of hammers and the swishing of saws as men construct his future execution machine. And that's what happened to Lucky Bill Thorington.

Every so often an historian finds a unique story that hasn't been researched and written to death, does his homework thoroughly, gets the facts straight and lays it out for us. He does not do it for money, or fame or a Mercedes. He does it because it is what gives him pleasure, to learn the story first for himself, and then to put it down in words so we can be entertained or informed.

Such a writer is not like a journalist who can go to living witnesses and look them in the eyes and ask them questions and discover who is telling the truth and who is a liar. An historian must rely upon the testimonies of men who are dead who may have been liars, and old newspaper accounts by journalists who likely weren't on the scene and may not have had their facts straight. Worse, any historian who tries to discover the details of the trial and hanging of a man that happened a hundred and fifty years ago, and doesn't have access to the actual written account of the trial, is in trouble.

Makley did have something to start with. Thompson and West,

in their *History of Nevada*, offer some information about Lucky Bill's hanging. They defended Thorington and said his hanging was a miscarriage of justice. Asa M. Fairfield, in his *A Pioneer History of Lassen County, California*, written nearly a half century after Lucky Bill's murder, claims Thorington got what he deserved. Makley decided to find out for himself what is the truth.

Author Michael Makley has done his homework and done it well. He has gone through the earliest records of Nevada Territory, newspaper accounts, testimonies of eyewitnesses, books and articles, and lays out for us what really got Lucky Bill hanged. Makley has come up with a fascinating tale, something like the Biblical story of Cain and Abel, a story of bad men who did something terrible and dark to a good man, and in the end got what they deserved. It is interesting to discover, that even in the primitive, wicked, hell-hole of early Nevada, Providence in His own time and in His own way, was busy setting matters straight despite man's interference. Makley's story of Lucky Bill's death and retribution is evidence of that.

Mike Makley's account of the life and hanging of Lucky Bill Thorington is an important contribution to Nevada history.

Carson City, Nevada
Spring, 1993

EXTRACTS

In the year 1858 occurred an event concerning which opinions have always differed, and that was the hanging of William B.Thorrington, popularly known as Lucky Bill...
          The Honorable Thomas Wren 1904

Lucky Bill is a 'character' quite by himself. He is an original; one of those geniuses who might have rendered a great and healthy service to society, if in his early days his attention had turned to something beside the speedy consumption of bad whiskey.
          S. (reported in The Sacramento Daily Union) 1857

The country had no handsomer or merrier citizen in it than Lucky Bill, a name given to him because of the fortunate result that seemed to attend his every action.
          Myron Angel 1881

Many stories might be told of his [Thorington's] good acts, that would put to blush those who make great professions of charity and love etc. but if a man gambled with him he was quite sure to lose his money. The narrator of this has often heard him advise people not to gamble.
          H. Van Sickle 1888

By sharp, and as many supposed not altogether legitimate practices this man [Thorington] had accumulated a handsome property, being the owner of several fine tracts of land and large numbers of cattle.
          J. Wells Kelly 1862

To me, as a boy, Lucky Bill appeared a noble character; grand in Physique, gentlemanly in deportment, neat in dress, kind in disposition and to his family, generous and charitable, and the best story-teller I ever heard. I have sat up all night listening to his humorous antecdotes and quaint talks and never felt a blush at any crudity in his language although they were related to a barroom audience.
          D.R. Hawkins 1912

Noticed along the road the gallows on which the vigilance committee hung "Lucky Bill" last June or July a reported horse-thief and murderer. Was astonished that the relic of such a season of popular agitation and excitement should be left to be harped upon by every passer by.
    Captain J.H. Simpson   1859

The writer remembers of reading a story written by a woman who said that when she and her husband reached Genoa on their journey across the plains they were imposed upon by some hard characters. Lucky Bill happened to notice it and he drove away their tormentors and helped them continue on their journey. She ended her story by calling the vengence of Heaven down upon the heads of those who hanged him.
    A.M. Fairfield   1916

Now whether it was just a put-up job to get rid of Lucky Bill, I don't know. Dad always told me that Lucky Bill wasn't the character that they figured him out. He always tried to do good for somebody, but he was a gambler, you know.
    Harry Hawkins   1966

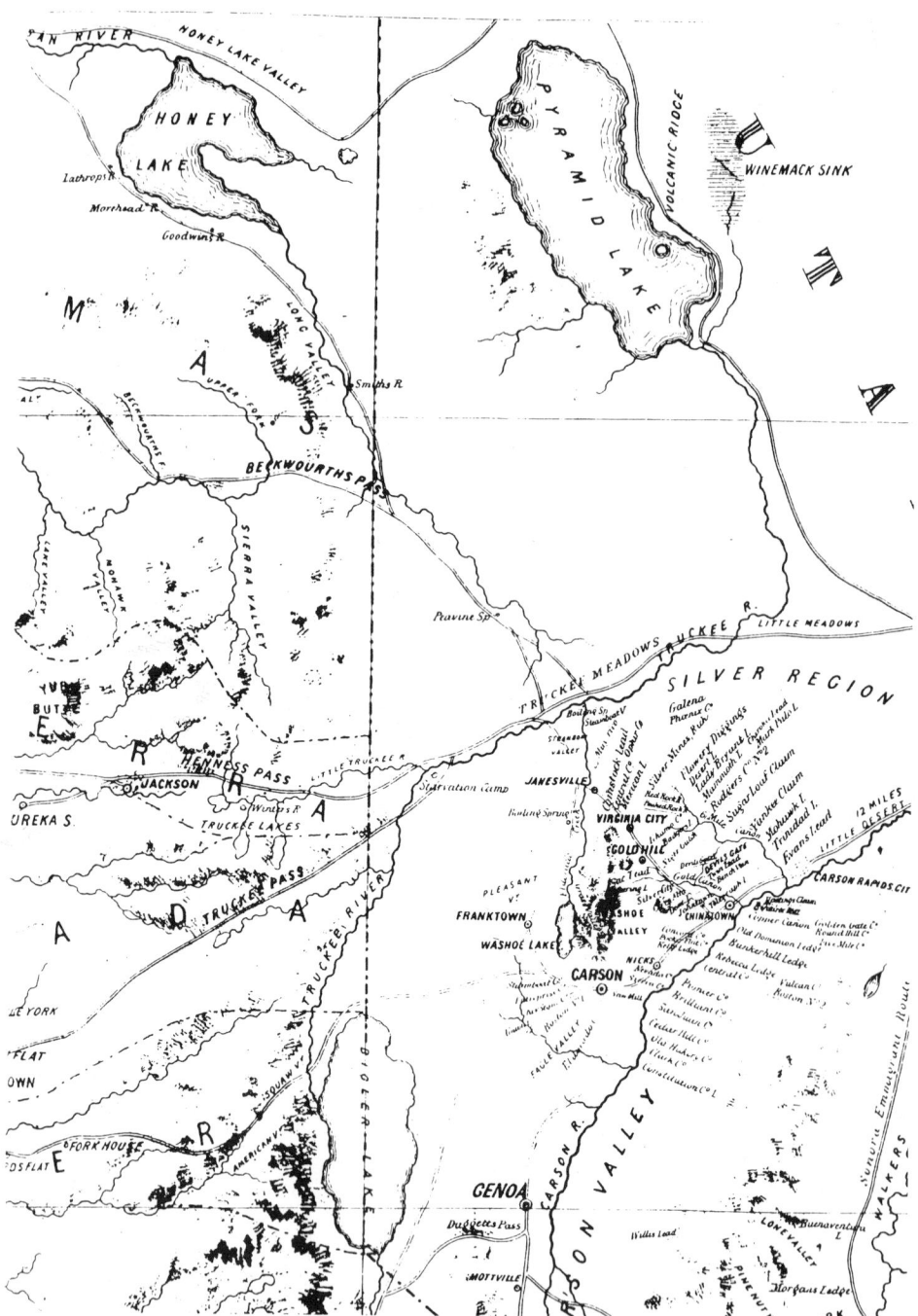

A map of the Washoe Mining Region drawn in 1860. It shows Honey Lake to the north, Genoa to the south--a two or three day ride on horseback. Note that Lake Tahoe was known as Lake Bigler. Courtesy Nevada Historical Society.

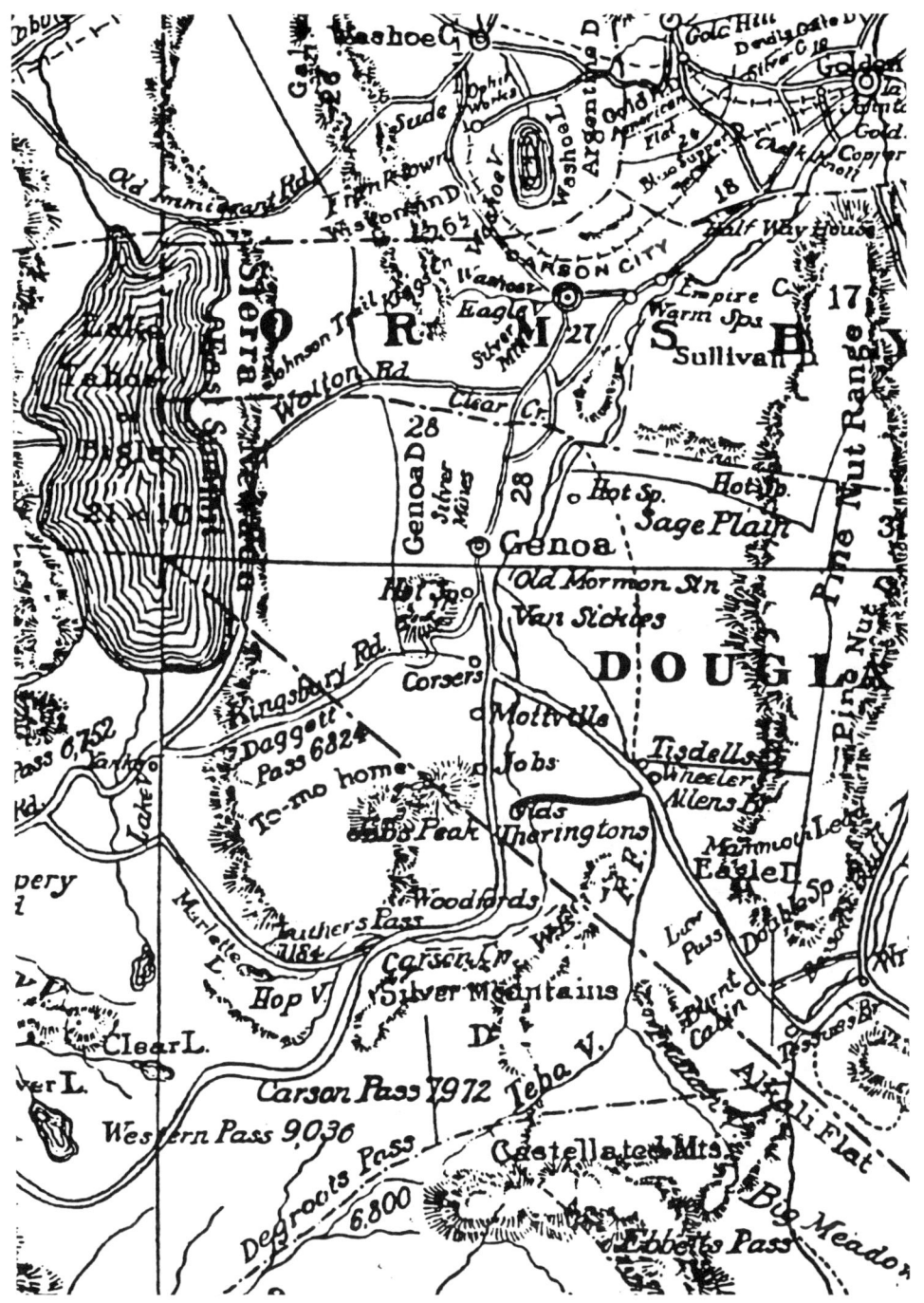

Degroots map of Nevada Territory, 1863. In the middle of the map the emigrant trail runs through Genoa, past Van Sickle's, Olds' and Thorington's. Courtesy Nevada Historical Society.

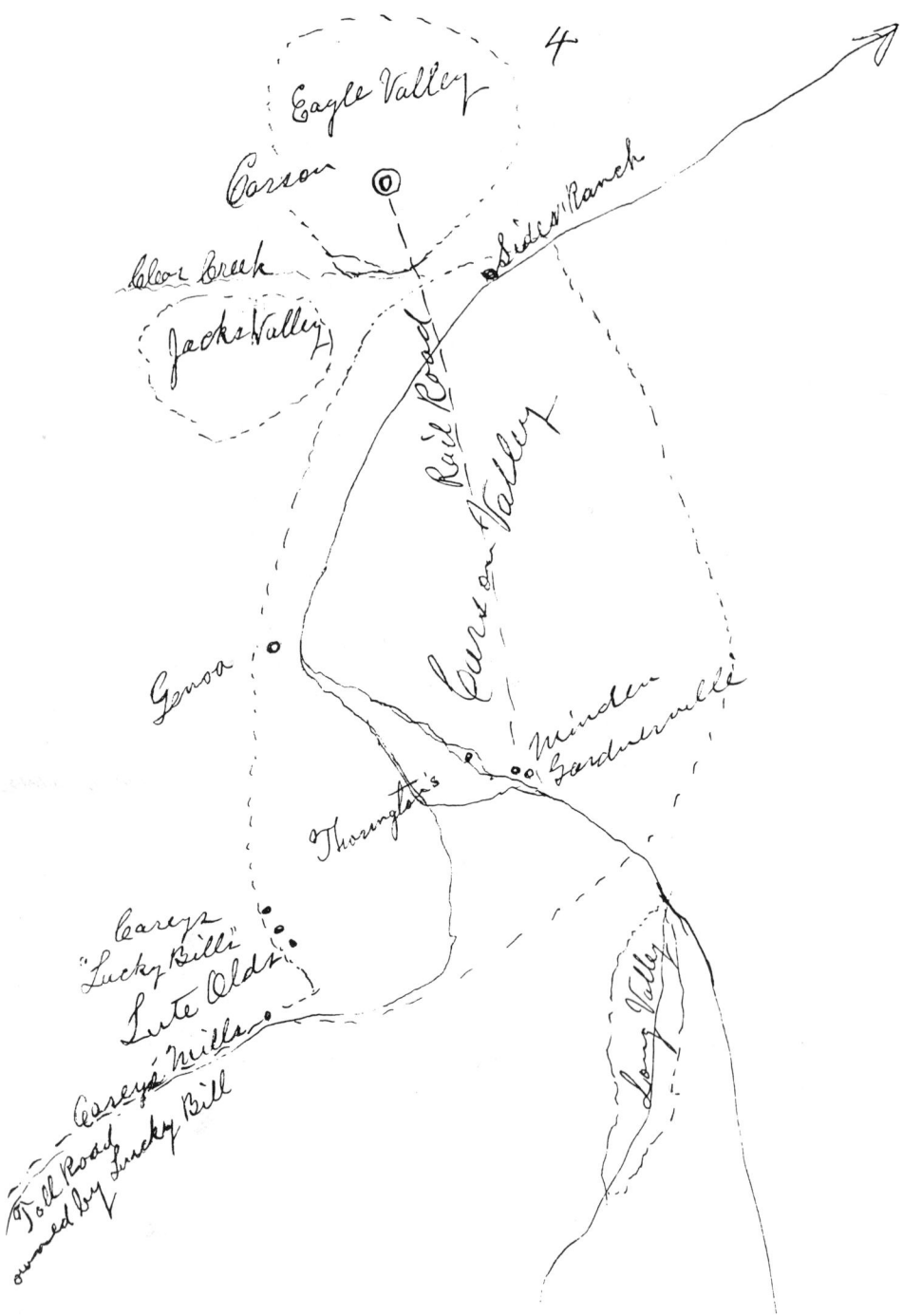

A map drawn by D.R. Hawkins in 1912 showing two of Thorington's ranches, Olds', Cary's, Clear Creek and Sides' ranch where Lucky Bill was hanged. Courtesy California Section, California State Library.

A scene from Carson Valley in the twentieth century. Courtesy Nevada Historical Society.

16 The Hanging of Lucky Bill

Note: Quoted materials in the text are printed in their original form without corrections in capitalization, punctuation or spelling. Where necessary, clarifications have been placed in brackets.

Chapter One

CARSON VALLEY

In the 1850's pioneers following the emigrant trail to California suffered many hardships. The worst came on the journey's last leg. After two or three months of travel, driving now exhausted teams, they came to the Great Basin and the meandering Humboldt River. In his book *Forty Niners* Archer Butler Hulbert wrote: "Someone said that the Humboldt was filled with what the Lord had left over when He made the world and what the Devil wouldn't take to fix up hell." For three hundred monotonous miles emigrants rode on hillsides above the bogs and swamps that border the Humboldt. When they reached the Humboldt sink they traded the brackish waters for a worse hardship: no water at all. In the Forty Mile Desert water and grass were replaced by sand. The crossing became thick with parts of failed wagons, remains of animals and shallow, simply marked graves. From this nightmare the trail led into what certainly must have seemed the portal to the promised land: Carson Valley.

The valley is a vast expanse of grass at the base of the eastern Sierra Nevadas. It is dissected by the Carson River. Cottonwoods which line the river were embraced and blessed by emigrants seeing their first shade trees in 1,000 miles. Steep mountain walls and jagged peaks border the valley on two sides. From these mountains snow-fed streams run into the Carson. It is also in the mountains that the winds gather. With bothersome frequency violent winds thunder across the valley and up into tiers of low rolling mounds called the Pine Nut Mountains.

Carson Valley's sky is pristine, broken only by hawks and occasional clouds from the California coast. The smells of the valley vary, from the vanilla scent of the jeffery pines along the mountains to the bittersweet sage after a rain or the spring earth turned by farmers and their new-mown hay. But, the prevailing smell is that of cattle. The valley has so much grass and water that

18   The Hanging of Lucky Bill

for a century and a half it has rivaled any in the west for raising cattle. Although beginning in the 1970's developers began exploiting it with tracts of urbanization, the valley still has many ranches, wild surroundings and much of its original grandeur.

Before 1850 the valley was home to antelope, deer and the Washoe Indians who had hunted and harvested in it over thousands of years. As early as 1839 Christopher "Kit" Carson is believed to have explored and trapped there. The valley, the river, a nearby pass and in the adjacent valley the capital of Nevada, are all named for him.

At the head of Carson Valley, close beneath the towering Sierras, is Nevada's first settlement. First known as Mormon Station then Genoa, it was permanently settled in July of 1851 by sixteen Mormons, led by John Reese. Reese developed a trading post, which soon included a blacksmith shop and, thanks to Thomas Knott, a non-Mormon millwright, a flouring and saw mill. Settlers also started ranches on adjacent pieces of land and in Eagle Valley and Washoe Valley to the north.

In November of 1851 the settlers held meetings to organize a squatter's government. The key resolutions adopted provided for the survey of land claims and the election of a magistrate and sheriff. In March of 1852 Utah, which had jurisdiction over the territory, created seven new counties in what would come to be known as Nevada. The settlers of Carson Valley paid no attention; hundreds of miles from Utah, they were managing their own affairs.

On December 1, 1852, John Reese (who, now, apparently because of his role as leading citizen, had begun calling himself "Colonel") filed the first land claim. Dozens followed.

There was little law in the territory. "Might makes right" and treachery seem to have been the controlling influences. As early as 1850 an emigrant, John Wood, identified the valleys along the Carson River as full of risks. In his diary he wrote: "All kinds of roguery is going on here; men are doing nothing else but steal horses, cattle, and mules."

Early settler, Henry Van Sickle, recalled one of the first cases in the valley: "A man owning a little trading post on Clear Creek where Lucky Bill was subsequently tried & hung, was assaulted by a intoxicated man by name J. L. Barnard, who attempted to ride his horse into his place of business and upon being requested by owner John L Dorn to refrain, and refusing got exasperated... borrowed a pistol and was coming toward Dorn's place of business, when within 15 ft of the door, with cocked pistol, Dorn in self defense shot him dead. Dorn was tried by our local self made authority and legally acquitted and fully exonerated. Several other occurences took place here, but it was a rare thing for one man to kill another except in self defense. Nearly every man either carried a gun or had one where he could readily get at it."

North of Carson Valley and east of Washoe and Eagle valleys, was Gold Canyon. There, beginning in 1851 just above the Carson River a hundred or two hundred miners worked the gravel with rockers, collecting gold. Their average take was between $5 and $10 a day per man. In the winter of 1852-53 a group of the miners decided to rob two supply trains traveling from Salt Lake City to Mormon Station. The train men fought back. A nephew of Daniel Boone led one of the trains. On January 1, 1853 The San Francisco *Herald* reported: "Mr. B. dared them to combat; but like all other mobites and cowards, they left the road open for the train to pass on."

On February 15th the San Francisco *Herald* reported that Mexican outlaws (referred to as "depredating greasers") were rumored to be in the vicinity. This, along with the miners action, caused the people of Carson Valley to turn to vigilantism. The Herald reported: "A vigilance committee was formed on Monday last for the purpose of ferreting out any evil doers; at least we are going to watch for them." No further mention of this group is ever made, indicating they took no action. Five years later another vigilance committee formed. Their actions would be of the gravest consequence.

The canyon to the southwest of Carson Valley, leading into the Sierras, had several names: Rocky Canyon, Big Canyon, Carson Canyon, Emigrant Canyon and later, Woodfords Canyon. It was a difficult stretch of road, filled with large rocks and a swift river. In 1849 J. M. Hixon wrote about the canyon in his diary: "We had to cross the river a number of times. The rocks we had to pass over in the stream as well as those in the road ranged in size from a nail keg to a whiskey barrel. Finally we encountered one as large as a sugar hogshead and that proved too much for one of our wagons. The hind axle of the wagon broke. We cut the bed and put the hind wheels on the forward axle and made a cart, loaded the goods onto that and proceeded up..."

In 1853, when Lucky Bill Thorington came to Carson Valley he joined forces with Colonel Reese to build a toll road through the canyon. The road, which Thorington would operate, vastly improved the last link of the emigrant trail to Placerville and Sacramento.

20   The Hanging of Lucky Bill

Thorington was already a wealthy man. Before bringing his wife and son to join him in 1854, he bought a mill at the southern end of Carson Valley and a ranch (The Fredricksburg Ranch) several miles above the mill. Thorington was known throughout Utah Territory and California as a gambler. He gambled in camp tents and barrooms from Ragtown in the Nevada desert to Sacramento. Archer Butler Hulbert wrote: "...but the most expensive thing here [at Ragtown] was experience in the thimble game operated by Lucky Bill, one of California's noted gamblers. Jerry Gullion staked his last ox and lost it; emboldened with whiskey, he lost his last dollar and five of G. W. Thissel's."

Lucky Bill had an agreeable personality and an attractive nature. In 1949 researchers George and Bliss Hinkle wrote: "His brilliant dark eyes were lighted with quizzical humor and with what seemed, even to his victims, a profound and secret compassion. This impression of great depths of sympathy, together with a certain large urbanity of manner, was his greatest asset — a semblence which a surprisingly large number of law-abiding residents of Genoa could only describe as 'nobility'....Lucky Bill could make a man count it a distinction to lose his shirt at a single turn of the card, and his rich baritone could make a barroom story sound like one of the Parables."

Lucky Bill engaged in all forms of gambling, but his specialty was thimblerig. Also known as the shell game, it involves maneuvering a small wax or buckskin ball beneath three cups while a spectator bets on its location. It is most often played to swindle spectators (the ball being hidden behind the player's fingernail and released beneath whichever cup is not chosen) and so a second Webster's definition for thimblerig is to cheat by trickery. Rollin Daggett was a newsman who later became a congressman from Nevada. While serving as editor of the San Francisco *Golden Era* in 1851, Daggett quoted Lucky Bill advertising his thimblerig game: "Here gentlemen, is a nice, quiet little game conducted on the square, and especially recommended by the clergy for its honesty and wholesome moral tendencies. I win only from blind men; all that have two good eyes can win a fortune. You see, gentlemen, here are three little wooden cups, and here is a little ball, which, for the sake of starting the game, I shall place under this one, as you can plainly see - thus and thus - and thus: and now I will bet two, four or six ounces that no gentleman can, the first time trying, raise the cup that the ball is under; if he can, he can win all the money that Bill, by patient toil and industry, has scraped together."

Thorington had a commanding physical presence. In 1881 Myron

Angel, editor of *History of Nevada*, wrote: "In form he was large, weighing 200 pounds, and with broad ample shoulders, stood six feet and one inch in height; his head covered with glossy curling hair colored like the raven's wing, was massive, with a high classic forehead, and large gray mirthful eyes, looking out from beneath projecting eyebrows, that indicated strong perceptive faculties. The country had no handsomer or merrier citizen in it than Lucky Bill..." This description is echoed in less Olympian but equally flattering terms by others who knew him. Henry Van Sickle, who lived near Thorington, said: "In relation to the character of the man Wm Thornton better known as Lucky Bill and who was quite a character in his time in this country it may be [said] he was a man about 6ft & one inch high 45 years of age well proportioned a fine looking man as one could find in a day walk, a gambler by profession and a man having many good qualities, a good worker at anything he ever undertook a better neighbor never lived near any man or a better friend to the weary traveler never lived." Another neighbor, A. H. Hawley wrote: "[Lucky Bill] was a fine manly looking fellow....an open free hearted man; tis true he was a gambler but he was a very true hearted generous man."

Thorington was a native of Chenango County, New York, having moved with his parents to Michigan in 1848 before crossing the plains in 1850. Angel said that his education was modest "due to the fact that his excessive animal spirits and vitality would not permit a close application to study when attending school in his youth."

Lucky Bill's wife, Maria, was described as "strikingly beautiful" with "coal black hair and huge brown eyes." Little is written of her, although it is said she became "a favorite in Genoa." Their son, Jerome (William Jerome), was 12 years old when he and his mother arrived in the valley. Lucky Bill seems to have been attempting to settle down by coming to Carson Valley. Besides his mill, he ran a trading post located for a time in a small brush tent. Once the toll road was completed he supervised it and his ranch; he loaned $23,000 to Colonel Reese, procured more land, built a house in town, brought the first fruit trees into the valley and dug the first irrigation ditches. At times, though, he may have projected the image of an idler. Emanual Penrod, who lived in Eagle Valley, wrote that Lucky Bill often said of himself: "never worked nor never will." If quoted accurately this statement was almost certainly a ruse, perhaps used in barrooms attempting to dupe a prospect, since it is contradicted by Thorington's Carson Valley neighbors and the record of his business successes. It has generally

22   The Hanging of Lucky Bill

been concluded by researchers that he was one of the most industrious men in the territory.

In speaking of Thorington's character Myron Angel commented: "...he was both generous and brave and his sympathies were readily aroused in favor of the unfortunate: or which in frontier parlance would be termed 'the under dog in a fight,' regardless of the causes that had placed the dog in that position."   Writer H. Hamlin said: "He [Lucky Bill] didn't inquire whether they were horse thieves or Mormon tithing collectors. His station was a rendevouz where the weary found rest and the hungry never were turned from his door." Something of this characteristic can be gleaned from an incident that occurred at his toll road. In the 1850's in Carson Valley, as in all the west, sheep maintained a notoriety: being perceived as an all devouring scourge. But, Thorington was never one to worry about how his actions might be viewed. "In 1853, (Kit) Carson, assisted by a crew of Mexican sheepherders, drove 5,000 head, brought from New Mexico, through Carson Valley and up the Carson (Woodford's) Canyon on their way to the hungry miners of California. Millwright Thomas Knott reports that William B. Thorington permitted the sheep to pass free over his toll bridge in the canyon!"

Two other events of 1853 would have ramifications in Carson Valley's and Lucky Bill's future. On August 19th the San Francisco *Herald* reported that an unnamed man traveling through the valley had killed one of his employees in a fit of rage. The murder was committed in cold blood and was witnessed by several onlookers. The man was taken to Placerville but, "he was set at liberty, because the laws and courts of California have no jurisdiction over offences, however flagrant, that may be committed east of the mountains." The paper concluded: "As a consequence, nothing prevents it [Carson Valley] being the rendezvous and refuge of robbers and murderers..." Despite the efforts of its settlers Carson Valley was considered a refuge for outlaws throughout the 1850's. This would count against Lucky Bill who, it was said, respected outlaws more than those who would betray an outlaw "if they had been asked for protection by the criminal."

The second incident involved Indians versus whites heightening ill feelings and raising further the demand by some for stringent law and order. On New Year's eve 1853 there was a dance held in the upstairs of a log store at the mouth of Gold Canyon. Nearly all the men in the territory were present, perhaps one hundred and fifty, and three quarters of all the women: nine. Despite the odds the dance was a success; too much so, perhaps, for during the revelry Washoe Indians drove off the celebrants' horses. The stock was eventually recovered "except two," as Angel described it; "that had been killed by the Indians for eating, at a general barbecue at Chalk Hill."

With government, outlaws and Indian relations all becoming problems inside the valley, another was raised outside. In 1852 the Mormon Church announced the long rumored revelation of Joseph Smith and officially accepted polygamy as part of its religion. The ruling stirred hateful fervor in Carson Valley, and became another of the issues which would lead to the hanging at Clear Creek.

Chapter Two

1854 and 1855

Situated on the emigrant trail, at the foot of the Sierra Nevada Mountains, Carson Valley was becoming an important site. With the settling of Mormon Station and several outlying stations travelers had a choice of resting places before beginning their ascent of the range. As the population of the valley increased the eastern California boundry line, heretofore only vaguely known, gained significance. In 1852 Mr. Eddy, Surveyor-General of California, had surveyed the area and stated: "...I was reluctantly forced to the conclusion that the valley [Carson Valley] was from twelve to fifteen miles out of the state."

Two groups of Carson Valley residents were dissatisfied with Mr. Eddy's report. The first felt the government of Utah paid too little attention to them; the second, too much (these believed any ruling by "Brigham's Legislature" was intrusive). The groups who wanted change were supported by the newspapers in California. On August 19, 1853 the San Francisco *Herald*, proposing Carson Valley be annexed into California, editorialized: "...[Carson Valley's] peaceable and law abiding citizens should enjoy a more prompt and immediate protection from the strong arm of our general Government than it possibly can while attached to a government so remote as that of which it now makes a part, the Salt Lake or Utah Territory." On January 23, 1854 the *Herald* declared a further reason for annexation: "If it should eventually prove true, that gold really exists in considerable quantities along the eastern slope of the Sierra Nevada mountains, Carson Valley is destined at no distant day to be an important point of inland trade." In 1853 some residents petitioned the California legislature to extend its jurisdiction into the valley.

The petition was passed by the state Senate but not the Assembly. Its narrow defeat stirred Utah into action. On January 17, 1854, Governor Brigham Young signed an act which provided for the organization of Carson County. The act stated that The Governor, "when he shall deem it expedient," would appoint a Probate Judge to divide the county into precincts and hold an election to fill the various offices. The judge did not appear for eighteen months, and the citizens continued struggling at governing themselves. (The disagreement over jurisdiction by the states would continue into 1856 when California decided to assess and tax property in Carson Valley. Utah already taxed the land. Most residents solved the dilema of fiscal allegiance by refusing to pay either).

John Cary, a non-Mormon and one of the valley's earliest settlers, chaired a citizens' meeting in May of 1854 that passed common sense resolutions concerning water. Two of the crucial resolutions provided that no household should be deprived of sufficient water, and that water should not be diverted from its original stream. Settling water rights helped create an order in the valley. But, the strange ironies found in all systems of justice were amplified in pioneer society. The case of E.L. Barnard is an illustration.

In 1853 Mr. Barnard was elected Justice of the Peace. In the first case in the territory his business partner, Colonel Reese, sued to recover $675 for supplies furnished to a Mr. Woodward. Woodward's company had been carrying the mails from Salt Lake to California. Justice Barnard found in favor of Reese, who was awarded $499 raised by the forced sale of Woodward and Company's four mules and various effects. Throughout '53 Mr. Barnard served with Solomon-like purpose. But, in 1854 he drove Reese and Company cattle into California, collected the money for their sale and never returned. On September 28 the San Francisco *Herald* reported that Magistrate Barnard had absconded with $60,000!

In July 1854 Colonel William Rogers, the most prominent citizen of Carson Valley, began a weekly pack train service between Placerville and Mormon Station. Rogers, known throughout the territory as "Uncle Billy," was a respected frontiersman: an old scout who had also served as sheriff of El Dorado County. Uncle Billy was Lucky Bill Thorington's close friend and business partner. He would be deeply involved in Lucky Bill's plight.

Late that summer three young men who held strong opinions and were quick to act came into Utah Territory. Richard Sides, L.B. Abernathy and John M. Baldwin were destined to be Thorington's enemies. By December they had purchased and moved onto a ranch at Clear Creek.

Lucky Bill, himself, having settled into the valley, seemed

always ready to help others. One afternoon in the summer of 1854 Thorington found a woman crying. She told Thorington she and her husband were being abandoned. Their partner owned the wagon and cattle that had brought them across the plains; they had supplied provisions. The provisions were gone; the expense of supplies and incidentals had been more than expected. The couple was broke. The wagon owner refused to take them further. Lucky Bill reassured her, telling her to "borrow no further trouble."

That night the wagon owner was persuaded to take part in Lucky Bill's thimblerig game. By morning he had "neither an outfit nor dollar in money left." Lucky Bill gave the loser back $15. He also bought him a new pair of boots advising him to "lite out" for California and never bet against a man playing his own game. Lucky Bill then hired a driver and gave the bankrupt couple the wagon, team and supplies that would carry them to California.

His generosity and his seeming inability to lose in gambling or business were making Thorington into a character of Herculean stature. After telling the above anecdote and one other, Myron Angel said: "Numerous incidents of generosity like these are remembered by the early settlers of Nevada of this strange frontiersman, many of whose impulses were such as ennoble men." In 1904 The Honorable Thomas Wren enlarged upon Angel's comment, saying: "Hundreds of instances are given showing his [Thorington's] generosity and bravery. Many emigrants who stopped at Mormon Station had occasion to bless him for his kindness."

On September 9, 1854 Colonel John Reese signed over "to Mr. William B. Thorington all the following property; To wit. — all the Ranch and furniture..." including the grain and hay raised on the Ranch that season, eight yoke of work cattle, one cow, ten head of horses, sixty head of hogs, seventy chickens, all farming and blacksmithing tools, the dry goods, groceries and hardware in the store, all household furniture and cooking utensils, his claim to the Eagle Ranch at Eagle Valley and one half of the Carson Valley Bridge and Old Emigrant Road. The property was given to Lucky Bill to satisfy a loan of $23,000 that was to have been repaid upon Judge Barnard's sale of Reese cattle in California. This transaction, although nearly bankrupting Reese, did not cause a break in his friendship with Thorington (Reese reportedly spoke for Lucky Bill at his trial). But, Reese's loss caused severe problems between Reese and Thomas Knott.

Reese had not paid for the grist and saw mill Knott built for him earlier that year. In the transfer of property to Thorington the mill was specifically excluded. Colonel Reese offered to turn over property to Knott in lieu of payment for the mill. Knott was not satisfied. In light of how business in the valley was beginning to boom, he wanted the mill, itself. Reese refused. This disagreement resulted in two volatile court cases and a feud that carried down to their descendents.

Lucky Bill's legend is filled with romance: chivalry, adventure and a love triangle. Considering his heroic and eccentric qualities rumors about him were inevitable. In affairs of the heart they were widespread.

He was said to have had two wives. Sarah Winnemucca Hopkins a Paiute Indian who lived among the whites in Carson Valley, later recalled her neighbors: "...another man, whose name was Dr. Daggett, had no family; nor had the next one, whose name was Van Sickle. The next one had more than one family; he had two wives, and his name was Thornton. The man who lived in the next house had still more wives. There were two brothers; one had three wives, and the other five. Their name was Reuse." The Reuses were John Reese and his brother Enoch, who ascribed to polygamy. Thornton was the non-Mormon, Lucky Bill Thorington.

Martha Lamb was the second woman. It is known that she lived first at Thorington's Fredricksburg ranch, then at one of his ranches in Eagle Valley. The rumors about her continue to this day. Some say she was married to Lucky Bill, others that she was his mistress, that she received half his property when he died, that she was Maria Thorington's niece. Stories say Thorington kidnapped her and that she was induced to follow him from Michigan along with two other young women, whose parents overtook and saved their girls. It has been said that her real name was Martha Baker or Bucker and that she came from the Saloons of Sacramento. Another story holds that her relationship with Lucky Bill caused his wife Maria to go insane. Few of these stories can be corroborated.

The *Records of Carson City, Utah and Nevada Territories 1855-61* show that on October 30, 1854, a George Lamb claimed land in Carson Valley adjacent to Thorington's and that Martha Lamb sold the same property on November 11, 1859. Nothing is recorded of George Lamb's life in the territory. Neither, is there evidence what relation Martha was to George. It is only known that sometime in 1856 or '57 Martha became pregnant by Lucky Bill and moved onto his Fredricksburg ranch. By that time Maria and Jerome were living in a house Thorington built in town.

The relationship between Thorington and Martha Lamb plays

an intregal part in his hanging. It has been proposed by Arnold Trimmer, an authority on Genoa history, that it was the central motive. Trimmer's family arrived in Carson Valley one week after the hanging of Thorington. Trimmer says: "Information coming down through my family — that the real reason for his being hung was that Martha Lamb was his poligamous wife....and the charge of harboring horse thieves was an excuse to stamp out any evidence of poligamy following the leaving of the Mormons."

Martha Lamb moved from Carson Valley to Inyo County after Lucky Bill's hanging. She lived to the age of 83, dying on January 17, 1914. Her version of her relationship with Thorington was taken with her to the grave. Her obituary, which appeared on the front page of the January 22 *Inyo Register*, reported that she raised four children (the oldest named William R. Thorington) and "held the respect and esteem" of all who knew her in Inyo County.

On January 31, 1855 the San Francisco *Herald* reported that a memorial had been presented to the California Congress, again asking that Carson Valley be placed within the limits of California. But, in the spring Brigham Young's close associate, the Mormon elder Orson Hyde, arrived in the valley to organize it. An escort of thirty-five men, including the U.S. Marshall for Utah Territory, accompanied the Probate Judge. Their arrival was followed throughout the summer by other Mormons moving into Carson County. This movement would insure the Mormons a majority in elections, thereby setting up the western boundary of what they thought of as "The Kingdom of God."

Despite an infestation of grasshoppers, which had damaged the wheat crop, and Indians stealing cattle, the valley was flourishing. Sawmills could not keep up with the demand for lumber. However, the problems between the Mormons and non-Mormons, smoldering for some time, now began to erupt. On July 17th the *Herald* reported that the prosperity of the valley was being threatened by Mormon actions. The year before Mormons had repaired two or three bridges at a cost of $800. Nominal tolls were to be levied to pay the expenses. But, in July it was reported that $20,000 had already been taken in and the Mormons would not stop collecting. "Americans" were outraged, the article said, because the tolls were turning away many travelers. A public meeting had been held and a resolution passed to protect emigrants from "the imposition" of the tolls. Because of the new resolution, the reporter, a Mr. Montgomery of Ranch Camp, had driven his cattle across a toll bridge without paying. He had been followed by Mormons who threatened to sue for trespass in California courts.

The report did not give the names of those collecting tolls. It is certain, though, that Lucky Bill Thorington was one. He had operated the Canyon toll road since '53 and had received half the Carson Valley Bridge and Emigrant Toll Road in partial payment of Colonel Reese's debt to him. This issue helps explain feelings against Thorington held by several valley businessmen (he was turning away potential business for them and yet on a whim would allow 5,000 hated sheep to pass for free). Three of these businessmen later became leaders in organizing "The Committee" — Carson Valley's vigilantes.

In the same July 17 report, the *Herald* told how Brigham Young had sent 100 Mormon settlers to Carson Valley and was ready to send 500 more if need be so that the valley would not be annexed into California.

Five days later there was another report on the difficulties between Mormons and non-Mormons. "A violent animosity has sprung up between them [the Mormons] and the Gentiles," the paper reported. The term "American settlers" was again used for non-Mormons, implying that Mormons owed allegiance only to their Church and therefore were un-American. Incindiary rhetoric was not uncommon in newspaper articles concerning Mormons. The Placerville *Mountain Democrat* later labeled Mormon leader Brigham Young, "an arch-imposter" and "supreme dictator," calling his lectures "harrangues of fanaticism." The paper would call his followers "unnaturalized foreigners of the lowest class," "fanatical instruments," "thieves," and "harlots." In the *Herald's* report Brigham Young was sarcastically dubbed "the Great High Priest of the Saints" and a settler was described as a neighbor with half a dozen wives and forty or fifty children. The paper would soon report that the number of Mormons in Carson Valley was increasing, further skewing the balance of power.

Researcher Juanita Brooks points out that Mormon judge Orson Hyde had little enthusiasm for his job of organizing Carson Valley. He was fifty years old and had spent much of the last few years on missions for his church. Realizing the value of having him in the turbulent territory and also his discontent serving at the western outpost, Brigham Young sent a wife to help him establish a more permanent residence. "Learning last Friday that you remained and do not intend to return this season, also of your want of a wife, we... obtained the services of bro. James Townsend, purchased a team &c. to go out to Carson County and take your wife to you." The wife was Mary Ann Price, mother of one child. She arrived in November, becoming another source of agitation to the anti-Mormons. Believing the judge to have other wives, they saw her presence as a flagrant example of the Mormon leadership's disdain for monogamy.

Judge Hyde stilled some of this animosity through tact and strong leadership. He ignored the poligamy issue while writing letters to California newspapers explaining how the territory was being organized. He worked with surveyors to determine the exact position of the state line. On September 7, when it was found that most of Carson Valley lay within Utah territory, he called for an election. It was to be held September 20 at the county seat, Mormon Station. Mormons won most races by large margins. In another tactful move Judge Hyde changed the name of the county seat to Genoa "...in honor of the birthplace of Columbus." Henry Van Sickle, a non-Mormon won election as Justice of The Peace. Another electee was Mormon J. C. Fain who had been the county recorder and now would serve as sheriff.

On October 27 a special term of the court was held at Colonel John Reese's house. At this meeting water rights were addressed for the first time since the squatters government made its determinations. This time a decree was issued stating water must be shared and not diverted. But, it was further determined that once the river left Carson Valley eight individuals were to be granted "sole and exclusive right to take out any portion of the waters of Carson River which they may desire, in a ditch or canal for mining and other purposes, in the vicinity of Gold Canyon." The eight were all Mormons and included Colonel Reese, newly elected Sheriff Fain and Judge Orson Hyde.

A view of Genoa's main street a half block east of Lucky Bill's house. Taken in 1868. Courtesy Nevada Historical Society.

Chapter Three

MORMONS AND INDIANS

In 1856 the Reese versus Knott case caused conflicts between Mormons and anti-Mormons to escalate. Colonel John Reese could not pay for the mill but refused to relinquish ownership. Reese was a Mormon. Thomas Knott, the debtee, was a gentile. Early in the year Knott left for Ohio to raise needed capital. He left his son Elzy to collect the debt. Elzy, a handsome man in his early twenties, was a friend of Lucky Bill's. Years later Elzy's younger brother, Albert Adams Knott, said: "They were together in the ranch business and very friendly. Elzy liked to gamble the same as Lucky Bill."

On May 22, 1856 a complaint was filed by Colonel Reese with Judge Orson Hyde. It charged trespass against Elzy Knott, the Clear Creek Ranch owners — R. D. Sides, L. B. Abernathy and J. M. Baldwin and unspecified others. Apparently Knott had attempted to confront Reese about payment for the mill; why the Sides' crowd was involved is not clear. As the trial was set to begin rancor erupted into hostility with the defendents menacing the court. Judge Hyde ordered special deputies called to keep order. In the book of records the clerk wrote: "In consequence of the threatening and hostile attitude assumed by the defence the court thought proper to issue an order to summon a trope of well disposed citizens, as a precautionary and prudent measure to repel any violence that might be offered: whereupon the following named persons were duly summoned and responded to the same:

J Hollinhead	H Mott
C Merkeley	J Mott
John Castro	Mr. Coper
Enoch Reese	S.A. Kinsey
John Reese	C.S. Daggett

W Fredrich   A. Mead"

The majority were Mormons. The Motts, Kinsey who was County Recorder, and Daggett — an attorney for the court, were especially prominent and well respected. It is interesting that the plaintiff and his brother also were among those charged with helping to keep order.

When jurors were being selected a man rejected by Reese was Lucky Bill's neighbor, Luther "Lute" Olds — later tried by the vigilantes with Lucky Bill. The defendents rejected Thorington, though he was Knott's partner, Justice of The Peace Henry Van Sickle and two others.

Witnesses for the defense included John Cary, B. L. King from Eagle Valley and a Mr. Perrin, presumably Solomon Perrin, an attorney for the court. Testimony and proceedings went unchronicled (an indication that the court's precautions had quelled any violence). The finding was recorded: for the plaintiff, Colonel Reese. The defendants were fined $454. They now became the most adamant anti-Mormons in the valley.

Even with Elzy Knott as one of the defendents it was not strange that the defense rejected Lucky Bill as a juror. It marks the distinct split of the citizenry into two factions. Lucky Bill was a friend of Reese and almost certainly had already had a business dispute with the anti-Mormons over tolls roads. Too, he and Justice of The Peace Van Sickle were relative old timers who enjoyed favorable relations with the Mormons (this, despite the fact that Orson Hyde and other Mormon elders disapproved of Lucky Bill, believing "he 'demoralized' members of the church who stopped paying tithing"). More significantly, Knott's codefendents, Sides, Abernathy and Baldwin, were Lucky Bill's enemies. Two years later, they, along with defense witnesses — Cary and King, would play key roles in his arrest and trial (by that time they also were enemies of Elzy Knott, who hid from them after Thorington's arrest). And, hearsay evidence which had originated with Solomon Perrin would be the crucial evidence used to convict Lucky Bill.

As for the resolution of the Knotts' case against Reese, a year and a half later Elzy won a $20,000 judgement. But, even in 1860, as reported in the April 3 San Francisco *Herald*, final settlement was pending. Because of which the whole town of Genoa was under attachment and lots could not be transferred.

In July 1856 a train of one hundred families arrived in Carson Valley from Salt Lake City. They came to farm and do missionary work, but they also came to insure the Mormons would win elections. In a vote on August 4 seven positions were contested, including a Justice of The Peace and two constables. All went to Mormons.

C.W. Drummond, District Judge of the Territory of Utah, had accompanied the new settlers. He was a traveling officer of the court, appointed by President Pierce. He had come to hold a session of the Territorial District Court. Using the loft of the Mott's barn he drew together a grand jury of twenty-three men.

Although a catalogue of complaints ranging from robbery and horsethieving to concubinage and gambling had previously been compiled, only two indictments were brought. Neither resulted in a conviction. It has been suggested that skeletons in the closets of the jury members may have prompted their merciful determinations. Whether or not this was the case, they obviously resisted Judge Drummond's authority. At one time he threatened "to iron" (jail) the grand jurors themselves for willful contempt. After six weeks of futility the official gave up, riding off to California. Judge Drummond never returned and no successor made his way into the territory for three years.

A month and a half after Judge Drummond's departure, Judge Orson Hyde was called back to Salt Lake City. This was the first sign that power in the valley would shift. The Mormons were in control, but difficulties were mounting. The opposition to Judge Drummand had mirrored that toward Hyde, himself. Hyde said that resistance to his jurisdiction had been unceasing "in almost every form, both trivial and important, open and secret." Action against him had included vocal assistance for the dissenters from the newspapers in California. This support coupled with the defiance of the Sides' crowd would eventually lead to open rebellion.

Until the white man came in 1850 the western part of the Great Basin, including Carson, Eagle and Washoe valleys, was shared by two Indian tribes, the Washoe and the Paiute. The valleys to the east were the domain of the Shoshone. Because each of these tribes traveled over large areas to gather and hunt, each people's territory could be exploited by the others without raising undue hostility. In fact, because the Washoe and Paiute were peaceful neighbors and because both were hunters and gatherers early white explorers seem not to have differentiated between them. The Washoe, though, whose population density was very low, were dissimilar in that they were seldom seen in groups larger than a family. They numbered perhaps 3,000 in 1850 but rarely, if ever, came together as a clan in a single place. Except in the spring, when fishing at Lake Tahoe provided plentiful bounty, resources demanded that the Washoe work, live and travel, in small groups.

The earliest recorded meetings between whites and Indians in the Great Basin reflect a determination by whites to act decisively. Attrocities committed by both Indians and white mountain men in the Rocky Mountains of the 1820's and 30's set the stage for brutality. In 1832 celebrated trapper Joe Meek shot and killed a Shoshone at the headwaters of the Humboldt River because the Indian "looked as if he might" steal traps. The following year Joseph Walker, with Meek in his party, led an expedition that had occasion to confront a great number of "curious" Indians. The white men knew there was no help if they became surrounded, believing: "the country we were in was swarming with hostile savages, sufficient in number to devour us." For this reason Walker allowed his men to attack. They killed twenty-five and caused the rest to flee "howling and whining piteously." The Indians had not raised nor launched any weapon.

Still, in the 1840's most meetings between whites and the Indians of western Utah Territory were peaceful. Indians provided directions and useful information to the Bidwell-Bartleson party of 1841 and Kit Carson and the Fremont expedition in 1844. But, by the 1850's the Indians no longer welcomed the white men. Incidents had occured wherein Indian women were raped and men and women killed. The whites perpetuated such crimes for real or imagined transgressions or to gain reputations. In 1851 future notorious Danite Bill Hickman and five associates killed several braves and squaws, scalping the former, merely for "the pleasure that killing of redskins afforded." Too, more and more whites had decided to stay in the valleys. They claimed and fenced valuable meadows and gathering land, cut down pine nut orchards for lumber or firewood, and exploited the game and fish; the total of which had provided the Indian livelihood.

In the 1850's the Shoshone engaged in a series of retaliatory attacks against whites. The Paiutes, under the leadership of Winnemucca and Numaga, formed war bands. Before this the Indians were held in contempt because they did not band together to fight. In his book *The Two Worlds of The Washo* Anthropologist James F. Downs noted: "Moreover, a people so devoid of national pride as not to attack whites, which many of the settlers fully expected, attracted the contempt of the invaders."

The Washoe would never wage war against the whites. Their

lifestyle did not lend itself to armed campaigns. They also realized that the whites' had power beyond their own. They viewed the whites as fearsome and unpredictable. The Washoe word for whites is "mushege." In the 1850's it was the same word that was used for fierce animals, and even into the 1960's carried the connotation of madness.

In 1855 the Paiutes, represented by Chief Winnemucca, agreed to a treaty of friendship with the settlers. The terms provided that Indians accused of killing or robbing whites would be brought to justice before the Paiute tribal council and whites who committed crimes against paiutes would be prosecuted by the settlers' government. "The treaty expressly disapproved of indiscriminate revenge or reprisal."

There were, though, further incidents of whites kidnapping, tormenting or shooting peaceful Indians and of Indians raiding and stealing from whites. Myron Angel commented that in the fifties "there were more or less murders both of whites and Indians, along the line of the overland road; within what is now Nevada." In May of 1856 John "Snowshoe" Thompson, the legendary Norwegian mountainman who skied the mountains packing mail between Carson Valley and Placerville, carried word that Indians had burned a cabin on Clear Creek. On May 3rd the San Francisco *Herald* said that the action had been taken because eight hundred Indians living east of Carson Valley felt the whites were interfering with their fishing grounds.

September 7th, news with a different twist was published in the *Herald*. On a mountain pass emigrants caught a white man dressed as an Indian attempting to rob another traveler. Seven friends of the robber arrived at the scene and six were slain. The last man was pursued into a small canyon above Carson Valley where three others, including a known horse thief named George Howard, had herded about one hundred and sixty stolen horses. All four bandits were captured and taken to Placerville. This was the first time in Utah Territory that an outlaw had been apprehended disguising his crime as an act of an Indian. There soon would be a similar incident. It would lead to the loss of several lives and grievously affect the course of events in Carson Valley.

Lucky Bill made a career of helping others. Sometime in 1856 three men stayed overnight in Genoa on their way back from the California gold fields to Illinois. The following morning one of them, a penniless old man, awoke to find his horse had died. He stood broken in the roadway watching his companions disappear back toward the states. Lucky Bill snapped his fingers after the departing horsemen and in an "inspiring and whole-souled" voice said: "Cheer up, old man. I'll show you a trick worth eight of that." A few days later the heretofore luckless man started out in a two wheeled vehicle filled with provisions and pulled by a strong roan — all given to him by Lucky Bill.

Grace Dangberg, the Carson Valley historian, related an incident that portrays Thorington in a different light. She told of an occurrence concerning her grandfather and Lucky Bill: "How the necessity for having a partner or forming a company was impressed on one of these men is illustrated by the experience of H.F. Dangberg who took up a claim in Carson Valley in 1856. On one occasion when he left his claim either to purchase supplies or to sell his produce — beef or butter — he returned to find Lucky Bill Thorington seated on the step of his cabin with a gun across his knees. Lucky Bill was indulging in a practice known as claim jumping which had been reported in Carson Valley in the previous summer (San Francisco *Herald*, July 6, 1855). The charming gambler, who also enjoyed the reputation of being a frontier Robin Hood, was smiling when Dangberg rode up. With his hand on the trigger he said, 'What are you going to do now, Dutchman?'

"Dangberg said not a word but vowing in his heart to recover his claim under more favorable circumstances, turned his horse and rode away. Early in the following year he went above Thorington on the East Fork of the Carson River where he staked out another claim. In this instance Dangberg was a partner in company with Charles Holbrook and Ben Mast. Forty-seven years later, in 1902, Dangberg recovered his first claim, which was by then known as the Klauber Ranch."

No other source mentions this incident, which apparently was part of the Dangberg family tradition. In the early records there is no claim registered by H.F. Dangberg until February 4, 1858 — the claim taken in partnership with Holbrook and Mast (but, pioneer records are at times incorrect and often incomplete). Assuming the story true, two facts are pointed up: one, Lucky Bill was no angel; two, in business dealings these men were playing hardball (and Thorington was winning every game).

There is no evidence that H. F. Dangberg took any part in Thorington's trial or execution, but other powerful settlers did. One Genoa pioneer believed that ill feelings over business deals were a large factor. D. R. Hawkins, who at age twelve accompanied his father to talk with Lucky Bill after his arrest by the

38   The Hanging of Lucky Bill

vigilance committee, was asked by historian A. M. Fairfield if the people of Genoa were glad Thorington was arrested. In a letter dated March 10, 1912 Hawkins replied: "Decidedly, no. Only his enemies Ormsby, Swanger (Ormsby's clerk), John Carey —Judge in the case — and W. B. Wade all of whom had had business differences with him, rejoiced."

Honey Lake was the closest settlement along the eastern Sierras to Carson Valley. Although it was a hard two day ride on horseback, the settlers of the two valleys saw each other as neighbors and allies.

In 1850 old Peter Lassen, having explored and trail blazed in the west for ten years, came upon Honey Lake. When he returned in 1855 Issac Roop and a small party had already been settled there for a year. None of them knew whether their valley belonged to California or Utah Territory. There was, though, strong opposition to Mormon ways and the Honey Lakers twice petitioned California for admission into the state. But, Utah included the valley when they created Carson County spurring the residents into an abortive attempt at creating their own state.

Emigrant trains and herds of cattle and sheep passed through the valley in the 1850's with Issac Roop's house being the only way station. Roop was a widower in his mid-thirties. He acted as arbiter, land recorder and, for the down and out, money lender. The Susan River and the city of Susanville are named for his daughter. Peter Lassen, for whom a mountain and county are named, acted as the country's elder statesman. Each man had great prestige among the settlers and emigrants; neither had material gain to show for it.

Life in Honey Lake Valley was easy: animals could browse year round and the rich earth produced without cultivation. Making a living from the soil was so easy that residents soon gained the nickname "neversweats." Still, Honey Lake was a dangerous land surrounded on three sides by Indian country. And, their valley, like Carson, had attracted a number of gunmen, road agents and rustlers who preferred lawless country. "The Honey Lakers wore six guns and bowie knives as necessary daily accouterments, just as they wore boots and shirts; and no man rode out of the valley, or even far into his own fields, without toting a rifle."

Honey Lake Valley seemed in a state of turmoil much of the time. There were few women. The men rebelled against those who tried to govern them from outside, squabbled with each other and battled the Indians. A.M. Fairfield told of an incident wherein a party of neversweats had pursued Indians who had stolen several horses and mules. They had difficulty recovering the animals but killed numerous Indians, including several innocent men and a woman huddled around a campfire. In conclusion Fairfield states: "Though the Honey Lakers brought back only one of the stolen animals, they made a good many of what they considered to be the only good Indians, and so were well satisfied with their trip."

In the spring of 1858 thirty-two Honey Lakers would thunder into Carson Valley, forming the core group that would arrest Lucky Bill Thorington.

Sarah Winnemucca Hopkins. Courtesy Nevada Historical Society.

Chapter Four

MAJOR ORMSBY

Major William Ormsby, after whom Ormsby County, Nevada is named, arrived in Genoa sometime in late 1856 or early 1857. He was a trader, who at first rented space for the sale of general merchandise from Lucky Bill. In October of '57 he and his brother-in-law, J.K. Trumbo, bought one and a half lots in Genoa; in January he bought a store at the mouth of Gold Canyon. He and his clerk, Samuel Swanger, also invested in land in Eagle Valley. In 1858 he helped Abraham Curry lay out the site of Carson City. In 1859 he moved there. He was a leader in the territory's secessionist movement against the government of Utah. And, along with Richard Sides and the other Clear Creek Ranch owners, Ormsby was Lucky Bill Thorington's bitter enemy.

William M. Ormsby was born in Pennsylvania in 1814. At thirty he married Margret Trumbo. Five years later, leaving his wife and young daughter with his in-laws in Kentucky, he joined two brothers and his brother-in-law in the 49er rush to California. There, the Ormsbys opened the first private mint in Sacramento. They melted gold, casting it into bars, rolling it into strips and stamping out dye marked coins with a sledgehammer. Business was said to have been extensive in 1850 but apparently was not as profitable as they hoped. They closed the mint in November of that year. Ormsby became a stockdealer and real estate agent and acted as an auctioneer. He had a strongly developed sense of right and wrong, and in January of 1851 was appointed to the Sacramento Grand Jury. In 1852 he and his older brother travelled to the states and brought their families back to California.

In 1853 and '54 Ormsby was a partner in a stage company that ran a line between Sacramento and Marysville. There is no record of his activities during 1855 and '56. It was believed in Carson

Valley that he was one of the irregulars in filibusterer William Walker's army. Walker's ambition was to overthrow the government of Nicaragua and establish a Central American federation of pro-slavery states. He twice led groups of mercenaries to the troubled country before being executed there in 1860. In the March 10, 1912 letter to Fairfield, D. R. Hawkins stated that Ormsby "had been a buccaneer with Walker in Nicaragua." In 1881 Thomas Knott wrote a manuscript titled "Reminiscences" in which he called Ormsby a "Walker filibusterer." Knott's manuscript was reprinted in 1947 by H. Hamlin who commented further on Ormsby, saying: "Very little is known about him, especially in Nevada. Mr. Knott called him a Walker filibusterer; who was one of the numerous lot that joined Walker's unsuccessful filibuster in Nicaragua in 1856....Knott had evidently run across Ormsby's trail in Nicaragua as he was there twice."

Ormsby had strong features: a high forehead, high cheekbones and a Roman nose. His hair was wavy and he wore his curly black beard neatly cropped. He was serious minded and self assured, taking leadership in all Carson Valley's pressing issues almost from the time he arrived. He seemed to envision what society should be and did not hesitate to act on his beliefs. He personified the progress that was winning the West. In 1972 writer Ferol Egan said: "He [Ormsby] was alive with energy, filled with ambition and sparked with vision." But, Egan also described Ormsby as, "a man of very excitable nature, a man quick to make a judgement," and deplored the self-appointed leader's behavior in one meeting with Paiutes, describing it as "blunt," "excited," and, from the Indian perspective, "barbarous."

In 1857 Indian troubles in Carson Valley escalated to dangerous, near hysterical, proportions. Culling reports from the San Francisco *Herald* and other papers, an intriguing, although at times less than factual, story unfolds. On March 8 the *Herald* reported that Snowshoe Thompson had carried news to Placerville that Indians had stolen a horse and killed several cows, other cows had been found with arrows in them "...one had seven." On May 26th the *Herald* brought word from Major William Ormsby that residents of Carson Valley feared an "Indian outbreak." Washoes had been caught stealing horses, for which they were whipped. The Indians were very upset and signal fires had been lit, apparently designating a place across The Carson River for a general meeting. The object of the meeting was uncertain but Ormsby said residents were preparing for the worst.

On August 18 there were two reports in the *Herald*. A Mr.

Hardin had given word of an Indian attack to the Sacramento *Union*. He was quoted as saying a wagon train had been attacked by thirty "Shoshony" Indians, twenty-four of whom had been killed along with a white man who was supposed to be their leader. Hardin also reported having seen the dead bodies of a number of whites.

The second story came from two men who carried word of an attack at Goose Creek with forty-five head of cattle being stolen. In this case, also, the messengers were convinced white men led the attack. They reported that both arrows and bullet balls had been fired during the skirmish and that they distinctly heard voices of three men who spoke English freely. Three white traders from the post at Gravelly Ford had disappeared and it was speculated that either they were now leading the Indians, or they had been killed by other whites who now were in league with the marauders.

In the same *Herald* report there was similar information collected by Major Ormsby and a friend, Judge Crane. They told of the organization of "bands of robbers" who had joined with Indians to perpetrate crimes. The *Herald* then concluded: "To exterminate them now is out of the question, but steps should, and we doubt not will be taken to prevent a recurrence of the scenes described by next year."

Five days later the paper printed similar stories of whites in league with Indians. That report included an incident showing how edgy settlers were becoming: while on guard duty a man had been accidently shot dead by one of his own party.

On September 1, 1857 word in the *Herald* was of another Indian massacre. A train had been attacked and six men and three children were reported killed. Also three more men had been murdered at Gravelly Ford and the body of one of the traders from that post, a man named Brown reported missing two weeks earlier, had been found. He had been shot through the heart and scalped.

On September 7th the Sacramento *Union* received word from Placerville that two "well esteemed" citizens, John McMarland and James Williams, had been ambushed and killed by Indians on a pass in the mountains between Carson Valley and Placerville. Williams' body was still missing. McMarland had been killed by an arrow, believed to be Washoe.

It was later made known that Uncle Billy Rogers' cabin had been robbed the evening before McMarland and Williams were killed. One of Rogers' employees had confronted several Indians suspected of the theft and thrown them out of the camp. The *Union* account said: "They (the Indians) became impudent, and the

44   The Hanging of Lucky Bill

murder followed."

On September 11th the *Herald* reported that the posse had found Williams' body. Although no arrests had yet been made there was no doubt that the arrows were from the Washoe tribe and the paper stated: "The Indians who committed the act are well known."

On the 29th the *Herald* told of serious trouble. The whole Washoe tribe had been painting their faces red. The brother of Washoe leader Captain Jim had been shot in the thigh by Uncle Billy Rogers. Eight hundred Pinto (Paiute) Indians were ready to help punish the murderers of McMarland and Williams.

On October 6th there was report of another attack at Goose Creek: two whites were killed, two wounded and twenty head of stock stolen. Uncle Billy Rogers was enroute to Sacramento with a petition to Governor Johnson asking for assistance. On the 9th two more men were reportedly killed by Washoes. Three hundred Washoes were said to be camped within a few miles of Genoa and they had declared their intentions to kill all whites in the valley. The *Herald* reported that the families of Carson Valley were without arms.

On October 14th a new correspondent, R.N. Allen, an attorney using the non de plume "Tennessee," wrote the *Herald*. He reported that there were eight thousand Washoe in the valley and that they were warlike and dangerous (Mr. Allen had just arrived in the valley and did not realize that he had overestimated by two and half times the entire Washoe population).

These reports, coming from various sources, many times reflected as much fear as fact. What actually occurred can be better realized using later accounts along with the "news."

The reports of the killings were true: attacks had been committed by Shoshones and some renegade Paiutes. It is likely that whites had joined forces with some small bands of Indians to raid trains and outlying trading posts. While some Washoe were involved in stealing or killing livestock they were not involved in the attacks against the white men.

Three days after Tennessee's report of the 14th William Ormsby reported that the Washoe had agreed to a treaty, greatly influenced by the fact that the Paiutes had agreed to help the settlers. About the same time Uncle Billy Rogers returned from Sacramento with a band of fifteen heavily armed volunteers. The presence of Uncle Billy's "army" also helped reduce fears and tension in the valley. On November 15th the *Herald* reported that everything had been quiet, and that the Indians were friendly if left alone. "Those who had been anxious to get up an Indian War," it stated; "have been

Major Ormsby   45

disappointed."

Several occurrences since the Williams and McMarland murders had drastically changed the settlers' perceptions of the Indians.

In Genoa a week after the murders Uncle Billy Rogers saw three Indians whom he believed had robbed his cabin. Rogers was known to the Indians as a brave and just man. He employed Indians and they at times used his residence as a rendevouz. In this instance one of the Washoe was wearing Rogers' stolen shirt, another carried a gun. The *Herald* of October 10th reported that Rogers confronted the men, sticking his finger in the muzzle of the gun so it would blow up if fired. The Indians attempted to run but were restrained. Rogers asked about the murders and the robbery, demanding the names of the perpetrators. The Indians would not answer. Instead, finding an opportunity they broke away. Rogers drew his own revolver and began firing, wounding one in two places. The wounded man was a relative of Washoe leader Captain Jim. Shortly after this incident, with the Indians dangerously excited, Rogers left for Sacramento to secure help.

At that time teenaged Sarah Winnemucca and her younger sister lived with Major Ormsby's family as companions for his daughter. Ormsby called in the girls' brother and cousin, Natchez and Numaga (also known as Young Winnemucca), young Paiute leaders. Natchez and Numaga identified the arrows found at the McMarland and Williams murder site as those of the Washoes. Although their manner of seeking justice would have been to wait for time to prove guilt or innocence, they agreed to help Major Ormsby secure suspects.

The Washoe leader, Captain Jim, was brought into Genoa. He admitted that the arrows were Washoe. Ormsby then told him that he had ten days to produce the killers, after which the Paiutes and whites together would attack his tribe. Sarah Winnemucca Hopkins (her married name) later wrote that Captain Jim responded: "I know my people have not killed the men, because none of my men have been away; we are all at Pine-nut Valley, and I do not know what to think of the sad thing that has happened." There was reason, besides Captain Jim's word, to believe the Indians did not murder the traders. Both men had been carrying money, but it was not on them when they were found. Their clothes and supplies, which Indians could have used, had not been taken. The Washoe had not yet learned to use money and so the robbery made no sense. Still, the arrows were evidence.

Six days later Captain Jim returned with three prisoners: two were unmarried, the third had been married a short time, with no children. The young wife and the prisoners' mothers accompanied them. The women pleaded with the Paiutes, Natchez and Numaga, to intervene, insisting that the men had not been away from their families for over a month, that they had been chosen by Captain Jim so the whole tribe would not suffer.

The prisoners were kept handcuffed in a small house over night. The next day, with townspeople gathered, Ormsby questioned them. Sarah Winnemucca Hopkins reported: "Some said, 'Hang the red devils right off,' and the white boys threw stones at them, and used most shameful language to them. At about three o'clock in the afternoon came thirty-one white men, all with guns on their shoulders, and as they marched my brother and cousin ran to meet them. One Washoe woman began to scream, 'Oh, they have come to kill them!'"

The crowd took charge of the prisoners reportedly to transfer them to a jail in California. Sarah Winnemucca's account continued: "Just then one of the women cried out, 'Look there, they have taken them out. See they are taking them away.' We were all looking after them, and before my brother got near them the three prisoners broke and ran. Of course they were shot. Two were wounded, and the third ran back with his hands up. But, all of them died.

"...I ran to Mrs. Ormsbey crying. I thought my poor heart would break. I said to her 'I believe those Washoe women. They say their men are all innocent...' Mrs. Ormsbey said, — 'How came the Washoe arrows there? and the chief himself has brought them to us, and my husband knows what he is doing.'"

After the shootings Sarah Winnemucca returned to live with the Paiutes. Katherine Gehn in a book about Sarah Winnemucca said that after living with the Ormsbys and interacting with whites Sarah developed an idea of their temperment. She liked them but, "It seemed to her they tended to jump to conclusions and panicked easily. They never took time to reason things out."

Sometime that winter Captain Jim came to the Paiutes to tell them Major Ormsby had informed him that the men who really killed McMarland and Williams had been caught. They were whites who admitted using Washoe arrows to make it appear Indians had killed them.

Chapter Five

THE COLLAPSE OF GOVERNMENT

Relations were good between Mormons and early non-Mormon settlers of western Utah Territory. Regarding the religious sect, Henry Van Sickle said: "...while here in the vallies they were a hard working and prosperous people. They never litigate on any subject but settle all matters in an amicable manner and to this one idea can be attributed much of their success in life....I always [found] their word to be as good as their bond."

Most original gentile settlers were like Van Sickle, living alongside Mormons without difficulty. But, by 1856 and '57 relations had soured, especially among more recent arrivals. Associations were affected by many factors. Colonel Reese and the Mormons who had arrived first had secured much of the prime land and created laws, backed by Salt Lake City's power, to protect their claims. The first non-Mormons to arrive had shared the wealth. Those who came later were outsiders, who had to be satisfied with lesser claims. The newcomers, who were commonly referred to as the anti-Mormons, vehemently resisted the Utah government's authority. They dubbed the original settlers and their allies The Mormon Party (irregardless of religion).

The anti-Mormons believed Mormon laws were unacceptable: particularly poligamy which they used as a rallying point against all Mormon ways. Newcomers complained that they were not dealt with fairly under Utah's justice system, that the Mormons received favorable treatment. They also felt powerless knowing that the Mormons voted in blocks and that Brigham Young had moved settlers into the territory to insure election results.

Relations between the federal government and Mormons in Utah were also breaking down. Feeling their rights were being abrogated, Mormons began defying laws. In 1856 in eastern Utah, an armed mob drove a U.S. District Judge from the territory. Non-Mormons believed the state of affairs amounted to resistance against the government. Mormons believed their liberty was being assaulted.

During the summer of 1857 in Carson Valley the entire fraternity of Mormons submitted to a new baptism. This led to speculation that perhaps orders from Salt Lake were imminent. Back on January 14, 1857 the Legislature of Utah had enacted a law saying all records of Carson County should be returned to Salt Lake County. It stated, though, that: "...Said county is allowed to retain its present organization....and may continue to elect those officers in accordance with the existing arrangements and laws, until further directed by Great Salt Lake county court or legislative enactment."

Orson Hyde had been hurriedly recalled. In order to fortify Salt Lake City, Brigham Young seemed to be preparing to reduce the boundaries of "The Kingdom of God." On March 8th a rumor surfaced in the San Francisco *Herald*. Snowshoe Thompson had carried word to Placerville that all Mormons were to be recalled to Salt Lake.

On April 13th Mormon elder Judge Chester Loveland appointed Lucky Bill Thorington to replace William Cary as Supervisor. He then adjourned county court until the first Monday in June. Instead, the court would not meet again until September of 1860, more than three years later.

During the remainder of the year a war of words was waged in newspapers east and west of Carson Valley. On July 15 the leading newspaper in Utah, the *Deseret News*, carried a lengthy editorial tracing the history of religious persecution. It concluded by counseling heathen "editors, politicians, Chief Priests and rulers" to "serve the God of all ages;" or if that was too straight and narrow a path, "do as Ganaliel advised: 'Refrain from these men and let them alone... lest haply ye be found to fight against God.' Acts V. 37 & 38."

On August 12th the same paper used a different tone, saying: "Rotten political pygmies have attained to almost supreme sway in the Government, and are fast trampling under foot the last vestige of unalienable rights..." The editorial went on to announce their purpose: "...to inform to 'the powers that be' that we are somewhat acquainted with their inhuman plans and designs, and shall subvert them so far as possible."

In Placerville, the *Mountain Democrat* was issuing a steady stream of anti-Mormon editorials. On October 31 it said: "So long as the country [Carson Valley] remains under the jurisdiction of the Mormons, so long will it be sparsely settled and comparatively valueless. Permit the inhabitants of the valley to establish a new territory next Spring and in less than three years it will be filled with a hardy, industrious, enterprising people." Another item referred to rumors of Mormons and Indians massacring a train (rumors that eventually proved true — referring to the slaying by fanatics of 150 men, women and children, since called "the Mountain Meadow Massacre"). If statements of emigrants were true, "and we have no reason to doubt them," the paper said; "the General Government will be forced to take some speedy steps to teach Brigham Young, his assassins, thieves, vagabonds, harlots and Indian allies, that Uncle Sam is powerful enough to protect his children and punish his rebellious subjects."

On August 26, 1857 the *Deseret News* had run an editorial by the ex-judge of Carson Valley, Orson Hyde. He warned that if armies were approaching they best beware, for the hand of the Lord would be involved: "He will send forth his angels and gather out of his kingdom all things that offend and that do iniquity."

By December 19th the *Mountain Democrat* was calling Brigham Young, "shrewd, amibitious, and unscrupulous" saying that he knew how to satisfy his followers: "He indulges them in all their degrading vices, sanctions with unction their lustful passions, and encourages them in every vile dissipation. They are taught to despise intellectual acquirements, to scoff at chastity, to mock all that refines and elevates humanity, to disregard all that the educated, the good and pure hold dear and sacred..." A week later, on the 26th, the paper said that in the event of a war with the Mormons Placerville and surrounding communities would furnish men: "Companies are organizing in different parts of our country, and a number of our young men, of the true grit, are eager to have a dash at Brigham and his followers."

This violent language was rooted in the fact that President Buchanan, believing the state of affairs in Mormon Utah amounted to rebellion, had sent a small army toward Salt Lake. Mormons now believed themselves under attack by "an armed mob of Gentiles."

By summer's end the rumors that the Mormons were being recalled from the western territory had been substantiated. In July a train of sixty-five Mormons had left Carson County for Utah. On September 15, 1857 the San Francisco *Herald* spoke of immigration into Carson Valley coming "thicker and faster" and announced that Mormon ranches were being disposed of to the newcomers. On the 22nd a great stirring of people and animals in the valley was announced.

On September 26th about 450 men, women and children, some

from Oregon and California, left for the City of Saints. "The property left by those people in titles to land and improvements upon it, in Carson County, passed for a trifle into the hands of others."

On October 6th the *Herald* copied a letter to the Sacramento *Union* from a Carson Valley correspondent. It said that Jared Crandall's stage service, begun in June (Major Ormsby was the Carson Valley agent) had allowed news to be transmitted faster. It also announced that Major Ormsby had visited the Mormons and that they left after dealing fairly with the gentiles. The next day Uncle Billy Rogers' account to the *State Journal* was reprinted in the *Herald*. In part it read: "They [the Mormons] paid up to the last dollar of indebtedness and left with the good wishes of all..." Uncle Billy continued, commenting on the saints' war-readiness: "They carried with them immense amounts of powder and other ammunition, and before their departure had purchased nearly all the revolvers in the Valley. Some members of the train had in possession as high as six of these weapons." (This mass sale of arms to the Mormons explains the valley's lack of weaponry reported shortly thereafter when the remaining settlers felt threatened by the Washoe).

There would be no war between Mormons and the U.S. army. At the brink of hostilities, Brigham Young and General Sydney Johnston of the army negotiated a peaceful agreement. But, passion against Mormons intensified as rumors of the "Mountain Meadow" tragedy spread. It also may have increased animosity against the faction of Carson Valley settlers who were seen as having aided and abetted the departed saints, hence supporting the government of Salt Lake City.

One of the men who left in the September train was Judge Chester Loveland. He carried with him the territory's court records. Mormon rule in Carson Valley was over.

Chapter Six

A DESPERATE FIGHT

Harry Hawkins, whose father had been a neighbor of Lucky Bill Thorington, said Lucky Bill at times beat emigrants out of their team and wagon, then gave them back: "Well lots of times, emigrants would come through and sometimes they'd lost their wagons and everything — horses and all. Well, he generally give them back to the wife and not to the husband (so they belonged to the wife not to the husband) and let them go on, you know."

On June 19, 1857 when the road between Carson Valley and Placerville was improved so that stage coaches could use it a man who signed himself "S" described Lucky Bill's hospitality to first time coach travellers: "Our entertainer did not like to be thanked for his courtesy and liberality, not on account of any false delicacy, but because, like Dr. Curtis, at the other end of the route, he appreciated the personal benefit he was to reap from the road when completed. Never mind boys, you're welcome to my free hostile reception this time, but look out! when you come again, I'll make you smart for it.'"

Some time later an incident was reported involving a pioneer couple who were being bullied and threatened by "hard characters." Noticing the fracus, Lucky Bill challenged and ran off the ruffians, then helped the couple continue their journey.

Lucky Bill also joined that summer with Uncle Billy Rogers and D.E. Gilbert to build The White House Hotel, generally referred to as "Lucky Bill's," the first hotel in Nevada. And, on December 1st he claimed 320 more acres of land. Never had his nickname seemed more appropriate.

In August, with the Mormons' departure imminent, the other settlers had rallied "for the purpose of petitioning Congress to organize a new Territory." The preliminary meeting was held on August 3rd at Gilbert's Saloon in Genoa. Colonel Reese chaired the meeting and a committee of arrangements numbering twenty individuals was appointed. The committee included: R. D. Sides,

Lucky Bill, Major Ormsby, D. E. Gilbert, and another friend of Thorington's named Orin Gray.

On August 8th a mass meeting was called, involving citizens from Carson Valley and all other settlements along the eastern slope of the Sierras including Honey Lake. Several resolutions were passed, the first being that a territorial government should be organized. The territory was to include the Great American Basin from the eastern Sierra Nevada Mountains to the Goose Creek Range, from the Oregon line on the north to the Colorado River on the south. The valleys of Carson, Washoe, Eagle and Honey Lake were all well within these immense boundaries.

A committee of twenty-eight individuals was selected to superintend business. Included on the committe of arrangements were Issac Roop, Peter Lassen and three others from Honey Lake. Judge James M. Crane, Major Ormsby's friend, was named as delegate to represent the proposed territory in Washington D.C.

A lengthy memorial was sent to the President and both houses of congress. It complained that the inhabitants of The Great American Basin had lived for six or seven years "without any Territorial, State, or Federal protection from Indian depredations and marauding outlaws, runaway criminals and convicts, as well as other evil-doers among white men and Indians." It continued in luminous prose: "We are peaceable inhabitants and law-abiding citizens, and do not wish to see anarchy, violence, bloodshed, and crime of every hue and grade waving their horrid scepter over this portion of our common country." Further:"...no debts can be collected by law; no offenders can be arrested,and no crime can be punished except by the code of Judge Lynch, and no obedience to government can be enforced..." R. D. Sides, Orin Gray, Uncle Billy Rogers and two others were nominated to secure signatures for the memorial. The Star Spangled Banner was sung and the meeting adjourned with "great harmony and enthusiasm" prevailing.

At the end of August, less than three weeks after the meeting's harmonious conclusion, an amazing news item appeared in the San Francisco *Herald*. The report was carried by a party of traders and published August 27. At this time there seem to have been three primary trading companies operating between Carson Valley and Placerville. One was operated by Uncle Billy Rogers, another by Jared Crandall (owner of the stage line for whom Major Ormsby had served as agent) and the trader most often mentioned in newspaper accounts, Major William Ormsby. The dateline in the *Herald* read Placerville, Aug. 25:

A Desperate Fight   53

By a party of traders just arrived from Carson Valley, we have three days later news from the emigration; also the particulars of a desperate and bloody fight, which took place at Col. Wm. Rodgers' Hotel, on the opening night of the establishment. The difficulty arose between several young men and Col. Rodgers, who had ordered them in a harsh manner to leave the room, when they were in company with a woman of disreputable character, formerly known in Sacramento as Miss Lamb, alias Baker, lately the mistress of the notorious Luckey Bill, alias Thorington. High words passed between Rodgers and the others, one of whom, named Sidus, knocked Rodgers down and left the house. Rodgers went out and armed himself. He afterwards returned to the room, when a man named Abernethy took up the quarrel and offered to fight it out in any shape. Rodgers drew his pistol and shot, the ball grazing the top of Abernethy's head, taking his scalp completely off. At the instant of firing Abernethy threw a rock at Col. Rodgers, striking him in the eye, and destroying it completely. Both dropped at the instant. Abernathy got up and completely mashed Rodgers' face by kicking him. The next day a party went to Rodgers' house and found he had gone, and the woman also. They then went to work and tore the house down. The whole population are determined to commence at once and give all disreputable characters notice to leave. Luckey Bill and his mistress will be the first to walk the plank. A Vigilance Committee is to be organized by these same parties...

On September 5th the Placerville *Mountain Democrat* published a letter from P.H. Lovell (later the telegraph operator at Genoa) disputing the traders' story: "The report of an affray here on the 20th ult., in which Col. Rodgers' name appears in no enviable light, is a misrepresentation of facts, reported no doubt by designing persons to injure our 'place' and some of its worthy citizens. The Col. is alive and well as usual, Abernathy also. The Hotel was opened on the morning of the 21st and is doing a thriving business under the management of D. E. Gilbert Esq. A statement of facts has been forwarded to California for publication."

The article concerning the fight in the *Herald*, however inaccurate in detail, allows two critical points in the Lucky Bill story. The fued that pitted Sides (called Sidus in the article), his partner Abernathy and "other young men" against Uncle Billy Rogers and Thorington was now in the open. And, it was a fact that Martha Lamb, and her relationship with Lucky Bill, was one source of the dispute.

P.H. Lovell suggested that the report had been issued by someone intending to defame Rogers and other "worthy" citizens. It is important to remember that the news was carried by traders.

54   The Hanging of Lucky Bill

Uncle Billy Rogers was in direct competition with whoever delivered the account. Since Lucky Bill controlled the Emigrant Canyon toll road and was a partner and close friend of Rogers we can assume he allowed Rogers whatever advantage he could. This, together with the earlier discussed toll disputes, suggests that the animosity contained in the report was influenced, at least in part, by business considerations.

The comments in the *Herald* that Rogers face was completely mashed and his house torn down certainly do not portray Uncle Billy in an "enviable light." The article calls Lucky Bill "notorious" and says that he and Martha Lamb, and perhaps by association, Uncle Billy, are "disreputable characters" against whom "the whole population" is determined to take action. In fact, as we have seen, Thorington had considerable support among the citizens of Carson Valley even with the departure of friends among the Mormons. Until this time the papers have painted Uncle Billy Rogers in a favorable light. He had been mentioned more than any other settler, with reports often commenting on his status as a frontiersman and leader.

The news that a vigilance committee was being formed by Sides, Abernathy and others and that Thorington and Martha Lamb would be "the first to walk the plank" is of utmost importance. In ten months Lucky Bill would be arrested by vigilantes and stand trial at Sides and Abernathy's ranch. Uncle Billy Rogers had been involved in "a desperate and bloody fight." It was a portent of things to come.

Chapter Seven

PRINCIPALS

In 1856 and '57 the anti-Mormons in Carson and Eagle valleys pressed to establish a new government. They wanted laws that reflected their morals. Their stance put them in opposition to the Mormons and successful non-Mormons already established in the valley. The anti-Mormons were unsuccessful because they were outnumbered. But, in 1857 when the Mormons abandoned the territory, control shifted dramatically.

The anti-Mormons' campaign to "civilize" the territory, now turned toward an obvious target: Lucky Bill Thorington. Lucky Bill had prospered in extensive dealings with the Mormons. He was a gambler who kept a mistress or Mormon-like second wife. He also befriended ne'er-do-wells, standing up to those who sought to dominate through force. Most damning of all, he believed his judgement superior to that of any government, putting him at odds with those seeking to govern.

When the anti-Mormons created a vigilance committee Lucky Bill and a group of friends created the anti-vigilantes. Researcher H. Hamlin said: "Both sides were armed and only by a miracle was a clash avoided that could have resulted in the death of a score, or two score men."

It is interesting to note that after Thorington's hanging almost all the vigilantes faded from the scene, while many of his friends remained (some of whose descendents continue to reside in Carson Valley). Of the principals in his life Martha Lamb, Uncle Billy Rogers and Major William Ormsby have already been discussed. Others need mention.

Thomas Knott and Elzy Knott

Thomas Knott and his son Elzy came to Carson Valley early in the 1850's. They built a sawmill for John Cary and one for Colonel Reese. A lawsuit over payment for building Reese's mill led to a fued of such bitterness that its "Mormon versus Gentile" aspect

56   The Hanging of Lucky Bill

carried down to the Knotts' descendents. In 1940, when asked about the early days in Carson Valley, Elzy's daughter Elzyette Knott Selby, who still lived in the valley, responded: "What do you want the real history of this town or Mormon history?" At about the same time Elzy's younger brother by sixteen years, Albert Knott (then ninety-eight years old), was interviewed. He stated that the Mormons had "marked Elzy" for death and "came to the mill after dad with a sledge hammer."

The Knott's first land claim in the valley was filed on April 11, 1853. They sold property to Lucky Bill Thorington four months later.

In 1857 Thomas Knott left for the east to raise money. He did not return until 1859, serving a term as Justice of The Peace for Carson City before leaving the region for good in the 1860's.

Elzy Knott was a partner with Lucky Bill in raising cattle. He had worked with Lucky Bill building the Emigrant Canyon road and was a close friend, each man's favorite pasttime being gambling.

In August 1857 Elzy and Mary Harris, a waitress at a Woodfords hotel, went riding. Mary was a beautiful girl who had come from South Wales the year before. They were riding along the emigrant road when they came to Justice of The Peace Henry Van Sickle's ranch. "...Elzy said to Mary, 'Let's get married. There's Henry over there in the field branding cattle.'" Mary accepted. The ceremony taking place then and there with field hands serving as witnesses and wedding party.

Elzy helped form the anti-vigilantes. When Lucky Bill was hanged he hid from the vigilantes. His brother said, "After Lucky Bill was killed Elzy had to hide out for several days with a bunch of other fellows....Elzy led the Anti-Vigilantes up in Genoa Canyon." Elzy's ill-starred fate would parallel Lucky Bill's: he was shot and killed less than a year after Thorington died.

Lute Olds

> *Down came robbers from the canyon!*
> *Down from Boarder Ruffian Range!*
> *Stealthy Slinkers in the darkness!*
> *Hear the story weird and strange:*
> *Came the horse thief gang one evening*
> *As the clock struck midnight hour;*
> *Blazed their guns that killed old Sawtooth*

Close beside his water tower.
W.F. Skyhawk

Luther "Lute" Olds had a ranch near Lucky Bill's Fredricksburg Ranch. He served as a Supervisor in Carson Valley and his residence was used as a polling place during elections. He also was said to be one of the Boarder Ruffians. His Cotton Hotel was across the emigrant trail from a canyon the Boarder Ruffians used to drive stolen stock into the mountains. Once the animals were fattened-up and their owners had moved on, they would be led back out for resale to others passing through the valley.

Olds, his brother-in-law — Issac Gandy and one of his hired hands Calvin Austin (a reputed horsethief from California) were arrested with Lucky Bill and put on trial by the vigilantes. Charges against Gandy were dropped. Austin and Lute Olds were found guilty of harboring an outlaw and were sentenced to banishment from the valley. Austin left. Olds never did.

Although Olds lived many years in Carson Valley and his daughter owned property in Genoa well into the twentieth century, Olds' reputation as an outlaw has stuck. In 1940 Elzyette Knott Selby said: "Lute Olds was a bigger horse thief than Lucky Bill could ever hope to be... I think the Carey's were in with Lute. Their ranches were all adjoining. My mother said Lucky Bill was better than all the folks around Horse Thief Canyon." Grace Dangberg also mentioned Olds being one of the Boarder Ruffians. But, as pointed out by correspondent Tennessee in the December 20,1858 San Francisco *Herald*, the only crime of which Olds was ever accused was, "entertaining those 'suspected' of horse stealing."

Lute had two brothers, John and David, who each had land claims in the valley. Together, the Olds brothers controlled 960 acres of prime ranch land. In 1863 David was elected to the first board of commissioners for Carson Valley's newly formed Douglas County. As will be told, he, too, later became a player in the Lucky Bill saga.

The Hawkins Family
Descendents of the Hawkins' family still reside in Genoa and the neighboring vicinity. John Hawkins brought his family to Carson Valley early in 1853. Three years after the family's arrival his step-daughter, Sarah Jane, married Stephen A. Kinsey, one of the original settlers of Genoa.

58   The Hanging of Lucky Bill

Hawkins' son Theodore rode for the Pony Express and knew Lucky Bill well. H. Hamlin wrote: "Theodore Hawkins was very friendly to the Lucky Bill crowd and probably was one of them." "One of them" refers to the anti-vigilantes.

John Hawkins and his younger son, D.R. — twelve years old at the time, visited Thorington after his arrest by the vigilantes. In 1912, D. R. Hawkins wrote about the event in two letters to A. M. Fairfield. Calling Thorington, "gentlemanly, kind and generous," he said: "...I had a great admiration for Lucky Bill and was sorry to see him in distress." When asked if the people of Genoa were glad at the arrest of Lucky Bill, D. R. Hawkins responded: "Decidedly, no." In his account of the incident, Fairfield omitted much of what Hawkins reported, failing to bring out the fact that most residents of Carson Valley were supporters of Lucky Bill.

Henry Van Sickle

Grace Dangberg described Henry Van Sickle as, "a man of many skills that were of signal importance in service to persons living on the Carson River Route." She then listed his work and contributions, which included: trader, blacksmith, innkeeper, Justice of The Peace, multi-term member of the Board of County Commissioners, county Treasurer, practical engineer, amateur banker — making loans on property, and early day real estate broker.

Van Sickle was a friend of Lucky Bill's, and said of him: "...a better neighbor never lived near any man." He called those that arrested Lucky Bill and the others "a mob" and charged that they held "a mock court" that "pretended to give them a trial." He concluded that, "the whole affair has a suspicious odor..."

Van Sickle gained renown in 1861 when he killed the notorious bad man Longhaired Sam Brown. Brown's "feats" included stabbing a man to death in a barroom then falling asleep on a pool table with the knife still in his hand, and wooling a judge (that is, banging the jurist's head against a courtroom wall until he fell unconcious). He claimed to have killed eleven men and thought to make Van Sickle the twelfth. After Brown attempted to shoot him, Van Sickle chased the killer, taking a shortcut to Lute Olds' Cotton Hotel. A writer called "Pony" reported: "Sam rode up very cautiously and reconnoitered the premises, when Van stepped from behind the barn door and literally filled his chest with buckshot. That was the last of one of the most noted desperadoes of modern times. His last words were, 'Van you ____, you've got me.'" The verdict at the inquest was that, "'Sam Brown's body had been filled with lead by Henry Van Sickle, and that it served him right.'"

Emanual "Manny" Penrod
Sam Davis' *The History of Nevada* says: "'Mannie' or Emanuel Penrod, was the last survivor of the original locators [of the Comstock Lode]....Mannie was something of a character."

In *The Big Bonanza* published in 1876, Dan DeQuille tells how in 1859 Peter O' Riley and Pat McLaughlin discovered what was to be the great Comstock Lode. The find was immediately disputed by H. T. P. Comstock who claimed that the land already belonged to him. "He [Comstock] boisterously declared that they should not work there at all unless they would agree to locate himself and his friend Manny (Emmanuel) Penrod in the claim." In the end, the discoverers agreed and Penrod was recorded as an original locator. It mattered little, as Penrod, like the others, bartered his share for a pittance, losing out on countless millions.

For a time, Manny Penrod lived on a ranch in Eagle Valley, near present-day Carson City. But, after the Comstock Lode's tremendous riches were revealed Penrod again took up prospecting, always dreaming of the next big bonanza. He worked a claim in Elko County until shortly before his death.

Manny Penrod knew Lucky Bill while each had ranches in Eagle Valley. He disapproved of Lucky Bill's gambling but acknowledged a redeeming quality in him. In 1904, using a style best described as inimitable, Penrod wrote: "But there is or was one redeamin quality in Luckey Bills favor, he was good to the poor and needy; he would always help a poor Emigrant and steal from all that would bite at his games; i say steal, for i think it nothing but stealing to play the thimble game; but the victim thinks he is only robbing the player, and so i don't know which is the worst, the man who plays the game or the man who thinks he is robbing the man who manipulates the thimbles and wax balls. For fear all do not understand i will explain..."

Penrod served on the jury that tried Lucky Bill. Fifty years later he wrote to A.M. Fairfield contending that it had been a fair trial. "...but was given every show with in the reach of justice. and Luckey Bill expressed himself satisfied with the jury, and expressed himself during the trial that his luck was gonen that the cards was stocked on him."

Richard Sides, L.B. Abernathy and J.M. Baldwin

Sarah Winnemucca Hopkins, in reciting the names of neighbors to Major Ormsby when she stayed with him, said: "The next house had three brothers, named Sides, with no families." The three brothers were actually Sides, Abernathy and Baldwin. They are first mentioned in the records of Utah Territory on December 20, 1854 when they claimed a ranch at Clear Creek and other land in Eagle Valley.

Sides seems to have been the leader as he is always mentioned first in records and reports. He also was the most active politically. In December of 1855 he was appointed county Treasurer by Orson Hyde, although he was replaced in August in the county election. In 1857 Sides was involved in the movement to make The Great Basin a territory: serving on two committees. In October of 1858 Judge John Child organized an election that he later discovered the anti-Mormons had sabotaged: "...but I have been informed since the election that it was the avowed intent on the part of said party, to elect men to office who would not qualify or give bonds, and thereby endeavor to thwart any efforts to establish law and order." In that election Sides, an adamant anti-Mormon, was elected Selectman and Abernathy was elected sheriff. Myron Angel commented: "The people payed but little attention to the results of this election, and although those receiving the highest number of votes were declared elected, the positions became mere sinecures."

In a three man race for sheriff in 1859 Abernathy received one vote out of 186. In January of 1862, in an unlikely comeback, Abernathy was elected county commissioner. But, he was replaced, without a recorded explanation, two weeks later.

John M. Baldwin is mentioned in county records with his partners in 1854 and '55. It is known that he was at the trial of Lucky Bill in June of 1858. He later told a man named Chartz that he was one of those who acted as guards outside the barn where Lucky Bill was tried, "well armed to prevent any interference." In the interim his name is not to be found. There was a John M. Baldwin who served with Walker's filibusterers in Nicaragua in 1856 and '57 but whether or not this was the same man is unknown.

What is certain about the men of Clear Creek Ranch is that they were vehemently opposed to the Mormons and the government of Utah. In December of 1858 at a meeting at their ranch any attempt by Utah authorities to reorganize Carson County was rejected. Sides and Abernathy — along with Major Ormsby, Samual Swanger and others forming a committee of ten — were appointed to take the county records from the elected clerk, Stephan A. Kinsey. Hearing of their plan, Kinsey sent the records to Governor Cummings in Utah, "...rather than that the Records fall into unsafe and irresponsible hands."

Sides and Abernathy were instrumental in the formation of the vigilance committee in Carson Valley. They feuded with Lucky Bill Thorington. They brawled with Uncle Billy Rogers. And, they were deeply involved in the hanging which took place on their ranch in June of 1858.

John L. Cary

John L. Cary was one of the first settlers in Carson Valley. By July of 1853 Cary's mill was producing lumber. In October he and his business associate, Thomas Knott, sold land to Lucky Bill Thorington. In May of 1854 he chaired a meeting regarding water rights in the valley. In 1857 he presided over an impromptu Peoples' Court to decide a property dispute about an area under cultivation. In 1859 a court was organized so the people might avoid resorting to a lynch court formed under "the excitement of some recent outrage." Cary was made judge. But, he was absent in the only reported trial (R. D. Sides' brother had killed a man in a card game and was accused of murder. Major Ormsby presided, granting the defendant bail and adjourning court. Sides eventually won acquital because of a lack of evidence.)

Cary's nephews came to Carson Valley to raise cattle in the mid 1850's, and at least one, Harry, worked with Major Ormsby for Crandall's Stage Lines.

John Cary had a ranch near Lucky Bill's and it is reported that they had business differences. Cary was the judge at Lucky Bill's trial but he left behind no accounting or impressions of the proceedings. When Myron Angel published the first account of the trial in 1881, John Cary had died.

Captain William Weatherlow and William Dow

Issac Roop and Peter Lassen were the leading citizens of Honey Lake Valley. Another man who influenced the Honey Lakers, serving as a leader in dealing with Indians, was Captain William Weatherlow. He was cool headed, preferring negotiations to warfare. He was friends with Chief Winnemucca and Chief Numaga of the Paiutes. He tried to insure that whites upheld their end of treaties, insisting that "justice for both peoples was to be the same." He is credited with saving many white lives, guiding wagons through Indian territory. He also led his men, The Honey Lake Rangers, on expeditions against renegades and marauders.

William Dow at times rode with Captain Weatherlow. Researchers George and Bliss Hinkle identified Dow and Weatherlow's lieutenant, U. J. Tutt, as "two of the ablest trackers" in Honey Lake Valley, and Dow is also mentioned by them as an "experienced Indian fighter."

Dow was involved in an incident wherein a man named Dexter Demming was killed by Indians at his brother's cabin near Honey Lake. Nothing is known of Dexter Demming but his brother was an avowed Indian hater. Ferol Egan commented: "Jack Demming, according to many neighbors, was a first-rate son-of-a-bitch....he openly bragged that whenever he caught an Indian traveling by himself, he cut another notch in his rifle stock." Egan described Dow's role in what followed Dexter Demming's killing: "Some of the men wanted to go after the Indians right away. One of them, William Dow, said that the Indians were so loaded with plunder that they couldn't be far away....It was his argument that if they headed out in a hurry, they would no doubt overtake the Indians by dawn and capture or shoot the whole lot before they even had time to climb out of their rabbit skin robes.

"But cooler and wiser heads prevailed."

Dow is a key figure in the Lucky Bill Thorington saga because he rode with the Honey Lakers to Carson Valley, and served on the jury at Thorington's trial. Moreover, Dow was the primary source of information concerning the event for historian A. M. Fairfield. Fairfield believed Dow to be a man of "undoubted veracity" and gave Dow's point of view when it conflicted with those of Carson Valley residents. But, by the time Fairfield was writing his history Dow was an old man whose recollections seem at times to have been colored by the selective memory of age. His thought process was faltering, also. Fairfield's book was published in 1916. On January 14, 1914 N. E. Spoon, acting as Dow's secretary, included a note after having written out responses to a series of questions posed by Fairfield: "Merrill: Mr. Dow's mind is not so good. He realizes it himself. he said you would have to get what information you wished from him soon. Come Again Yours, N. E. Spoon."

Chauncey N. Noteware
Mr. Noteware began his term of residence in Carson Valley in

Principals 63

October 1857. He had lived previously in Placerville, coming west in 1850. He traveled frequently between Carson Valley and the western slope in the mid-fifties, being well known and respected on both sides of the Sierras. Noteware was elected Surveyor for Carson County in October of 1858, beginning a distinguished career of government service. On the formation of Nevada Territory in 1860 he was appointed Probate Judge for Douglas County. He served as President of a constitutional convention in 1864 and from '64 to '70 served as Secretary of State for Nevada.

Chauncey Noteware's role in Lucky Bill Thorington's story is crucial. He transcribed the testimony of the trial. Thorington, apparently choosing Noteware because he would be seen as an unbiased reporter, asked him to record the evidence. After the turn of the century Noteware composed a statement concerning Lucky Bill. In it he stated: "The testimony was taken by C. N. Noteware at the request of Thorington, who declared at the time that he was bound to be executed by the committee, and he wanted the evidence upon which he would be convicted published." The trial transcript was published in full in The Placerville *Tri-Weekly Register* a few days after the trial. It was read and used by Myron Angel in his account in Thompson and West's *History of Nevada* published in 1881. Part of the testimony was reprinted from the *Register* by the Sacramento *Union* and still exists but the complete transcription does not.

Chapter Eight

MORALS AND MURDER

In December 1857 Uncle Billy Rogers was again demeaned by an unnamed writer in a California newspaper. This time it concerned the men he brought from Sacramento to defend settlers against the Indians. On December 16th the San Francisco *Herald's* new correspondent, Tennessee, responded: "I am very sorry to perceive that some evil disposed person has been misrepresenting the course of Uncle Billy Rogers. In justice to an upright and honorable old man, I beg leave to correct some impressions you have....In short, I know that no family in this place would feel secure if Uncle Billy's men were not here."

This controversy quickly died, for despite settlers' perceptions, the Washoe Indians were not going to fight. Within the month Uncle Billy had discharged his band and enemies could no longer use this issue to malign him.

By February 1, 1858 the San Francisco *Herald* was reporting that everything was quiet in Carson Valley. It was a lull before the storm.

On Thursday December 10, 1857 The San Francisco *Daily Alta* had carried a small item at the bottom of column one, page one. It told of the murder of a man named Snelling, the leading citizen at Snelling (the post having been named after him) in Merced County. The murder was known to have been committed by William Coombs Edwards, who had escaped. The Masons, of which Snelling had been a member, offered a $1500 reward for the capture of the murderer. Edwards had fled east over the Sierras.

In Carson Valley Edwards sought out a man who had a reputation for helping all who asked, Lucky Bill Thorington. He told the gambler of the killing, saying it had been self defense — something he would maintain until his death. Edwards wished to leave a sack of money with Thorington while he traveled to Honey Lake Valley, where he had friends. Without counting the money (there was upwards of $1,000) Thorington buried it under a willow tree on his ranch. Edwards, calling himself Bill Coombs, then continued to Honey Lake Valley to the ranch of W. T. C. "Rough" Elliot and Junius Brutus Gilpin.

At the beginning of 1858 relations with the Indians were calm. Most Mormons had left the valley; the rest would leave by mid-April. But, the feud between the "old guard" and the anti-Mormon faction was about to heat up. Tennessee wrote to the San Francisco *Herald* on February 8, 1858 saying: "Last Sunday week a public meeting was held here, for the purpose of promoting moral habits among the people — whether for that reason or from other causes, I know not — but it is very certain that [since that] time the people had more quarreling and fighting among themselves than they ever had before since my arrival. Today a man had his hand nearly cut off by another and tomorrow another person is to be tried for slander."

It is unclear toward which individuals the irony in Tennessee's report is directed, but an educated guess would include Major Ormsby. As evidenced by his actions in the Mormon issue, Indian disputes and territorial government Ormsby was a leader in such matters. Tennessee later called Ormsby his enemy and he was a friend of Ormsby's foes Uncle Billy and Lucky Bill (he would testify for Lucky Bill at his trial.)

On February 14th the *Herald* reported on the knifing incident Tennessee had mentioned. This report was carried by Snowshoe Thompson. After saying that everything in the valley was quiet Thompson reported that a difficulty had occurred at Genoa between two men named Thornton and Sisco. The latter individual had been severely wounded with a knife: his hand being nearly cut off. The Thornton in this report was Lucky Bill's son, Jerome. Many years later D. R. Hawkins wrote: "At a later date I saw Dr. Daggett on the same spot save the life of Cisco whose wrist was nearly severed by Jerome Thorington with a Bowie knife."

In February of 1858 newspapers carried reports concerning Indian troubles in Honey Lake Valley. On March 1st news from Tennessee in Carson Valley related that "Chief Winnemuck" had informed the people of Genoa that two white men, whom the Indians believed to be murderers, had stopped with the Paiutes. "At the time our informant left the valley," the *Herald* reported;"'Lucky Bill' Thorington was raising a posse of citizens to go out and arrest the two suspected worthies." On March 7th the *Herald* reported that: "Lucky Bill, with a posse of five or six men, had started in company with Winnemuck, the Paiute chief, in search of the two white desperadoes, of whom we made mention

66   The Hanging of Lucky Bill

in Tuesday's issue."

The posse that left Carson Valley was comprised of two parties: B. Cherry and Jack Howard in one, Lucky Bill, James Menofee and Ab. Smith in the other. They were searching for men named Stewart and Beasley. According to Cherry: "we (Jack and myself) did not go with the expectation of finding Stewart, who was supposed by the others to be with the Indians, but to try and ascertain something of the where abouts of Bill Edwards [the escaped killer of Snelling."]

When the group arrived at the Paiute camp they found that the men they were after had gone to Honey Lake. Cherry said: "...being at this time about out of provisions, we concluded to go direct to Honey Lake; we stopped at Crawford's ranch; during the entire route, up to the time we got to Crawford's, the name of Edwards had not been mentioned; here James Menofee mentioned his name and made inquiries concerning him; we (that is Jack Howard and myself) heard nothing of Edwards on the entire trip; next morning, we went down to the Know Nothing Boys and there found and arrested Beasley, Thorington said, 'Boys you take him back to Crawford's and I will go up to Sol. Perrin's, hire a horse and go up on Susan river and get money to buy supplies to get back to Carson Valley...'"

Lucky Bill left the others, riding to the ex-resident of Carson Valley, Solomon Perrin's. There, he borrowed a fresh horse and rode to Junius Brutus Gilpin's house at Honey Lake. A great number of the valley's residents were visiting when Thorington arrived at Gilpin's. Thorington sought out Bill Edwards, known there as Coombs, borrowing $15 and meeting privately with him beneath a large pine near the cabin. After a time Edwards called Gilpin over, showing him a letter Lucky Bill had received from Merced County (both Gilpin and Rough Elliot had been told by Edwards that he had killed Snelling in self defense). The letter said that people now believed Edwards was in Honey Lake Valley. Thorington had come to warn Edwards. When Lucky Bill left, Edwards rode with him perhaps a mile and a half, then returned.

At Perrin's, Lucky Bill offered to pay for the use of the horse, saying he had no money earlier, but had seen Coombs and obtained some. He got back to Crawford's at nine or ten that night. At Lucky Bill's trial Cherry said that when asked, "What luck?" Thorington replied: "'Good,' that he met up there a good many friends; that when he told them his name they were ready to give him any amount of money; that one man he judged had a roll of some $500, which he broke into and offered him one-half; that he refused it, only taking $15, which he needed; nothing more was said that night, only that the boys up there were a brave set of Texas boys and in this connection spoke of Elliot, Coombs, Gilpin, etc."

On the 14th of March the San Francisco *Herald* reported that Lucky Bill and the posse had returned after eight days without success (Beasley, the man Cherry says they arrested, is never mentioned).

It is possible that the first meeting of the Carson Valley vigilantes, who called themselves "The Committee," met while Lucky Bill was with the posse out of the valley. Historian Effie Mona Mack states that their first meeting was held in March of 1858. The meeting was called "for the purpose of correcting and amending the old laws of Carson County." H. Hamlin said: "There were 19 members of this secret organization that had as its secret meeting place an upstairs room of the home of a Mrs. Haines, later Mrs. Singleton, and later married a third time. The home, now gone, was in Genoa."

The membership of the Committee was kept secret but it is known that L. B. Abernathy and J. M. Baldwin belonged, as well as A. P. Squires and a man named Chavan. Evidence makes it certain that Richard Sides and Major Ormsby took leading roles and that John Cary was involved (on December 30, 1858 the San Francisco *Herald* reported a meeting that was held at Sides' Clear Creek Ranch, chaired by Ormsby, with Cary elected President. At that time a lengthy memorial was written stating that those present supported the actions of the vigilance committee at Lucky Bill's trial in June. "Resolved. That this committee recommend the people to sustain the award of the jury impanneled at Clear Creek Ranch on the 16th of June, 1858: pledged our lives to the faithful execution of its awards.")

Although The Committee was intended to be kept secret it obviously was not. Shortly after its formation Lucky Bill, Elzy Knott and seventeen others formed the anti-vigilantes (a number equal to that of the vigilantes). These men believed that by standing together they could thwart the use of force by the Sides-Ormsby faction. They were soon proven wrong.

On April 4th the *Herald* reported that Uncle Billy had been engaged with a man named Cloud in a "stone throwing scrape." Cloud ran pack trains with Ormsby, but the area of his disagreement with Uncle Billy went unreported. Snowshoe Thompson, who had carried the news, commented that the incident "amounted to nothing serious."

For the rest of April Carson Valley news in the *Herald* dealt with the coming and going of Major Ormsby's pack train and that of Jared Crandall. On the 19th Tennessee wrote that the last of the Mormons were leaving Carson Valley. For unexplained reasons, they had feared gentiles would not allow them to leave, but Tennessee says that Major Ormsby again stepped forward, assuring them safe passage.

Two altercations were also mentioned in April editions of the *Herald*, showing that neither the meeting on morals nor the formation of the vigilantes had gone far in improving social conduct. On the 18th it was reported that at a ball, about the first of the month, a fight had occurred in which bowie knives were used freely (no one was seriously hurt). On the 25th an article told how the previous week two men got drunk and "chased each other through the village with knives, stones, etc. and that was the end of the affair." The same article illustrated how business between Placerville and Carson Valley was booming. The arrival of John Child and Uncle Billy Rogers with twenty-five pack animals brought the total to 100 animals in two days. This mention of Uncle Billy was the last that would occur for many weeks. About the first of May he left for San Francisco, from there to travel down the coast on business. In mid-June when Honey Lakers joined members of The Committee to storm Genoa and arrest his friend Thorington, Uncle Billy would be far away in California.

A. M. Fairfield's *A Pioneer History of Lassen County, California* traces the early history of Honey Lake Valley. He lived many years in the county and he had an obvious affection for the land and its pioneers. At one point he uses a light hearted tone in telling how Honey Lake's early community was perceived: "You and I, kind reader, know that very few people excepting good ones lived in the land of the Never Sweats at that time but... Isaac N. Jones, long a supervisor of the county, related: 'People who claimed to know the country said that if they went through there they were likely to be robbed or killed, or at least have their horses stolen. One man in the train, who had been in California before, said he didn't believe the Honey Lakers were any worse than the Indians and he took the road leading to this valley. The rest of the train went on to Ragtown and up the Carson river.'"

Honey Laker W. T. C. Elliot was nicknamed "Rough." It is said he was called that because he came from the mining camp of Rough

Morals and Murder 69

and Ready. Fairfield commented: "He (Elliot) could be very polite and 'smooth' if he saw fit to do it." During the winter, early in 1858, Rough Elliot argued with J. H. "Blackhawk" Ferry, the town blacksmith. A few days later Elliot, who was younger and very powerful, backed Ferry over the anvil in his shop and "beat him up considerably." Later, when Elliot's dog wandered into Ferry's shop the blacksmith went after it with a gun. Elliot was nearby. Seeing Ferry, he jumped behind a stump and the two men emptied their pistols at one another. With Elliot trapped and out of amunition, Ferry took up his rifle exclaiming, "I'll get him now." But, before he could come out of the shop boys from the mill grabbed him, stopping the fight, "probably saving Elliot's life." His role in other, similar, incidents would lead most to conclude that regardless of whether Rough Elliot's nickname came from a previous residence or whether or not he could be 'smooth' at times, the name fit.

Fairfield describes another of the neversweats' adventures, this one in April of 1858 — a trip to Goose Lake chasing Indians. Five horses and three mules had been stolen. William Weatherlow led a posse that included Rough Elliot, Junius Brutus Gilpin and William Dow. One day at dawn the Honey Lakers found Indians around a campfire. "The whites immediately fired and killed all of them, three bucks and a squaw....They were Pit river or Dixie valley, Indians, but not the ones they were following. The white men thought, however, that they deserved their fate, for there were marrow bones and fresh rawhides in their camp."

Later, when the band seemed to have lost the track Rough Elliot and a man named Chapman almost fought over whether to turn back or not. Once the dispute was resolved and they ventured on, the neversweats came on a party of Mormons. Their train had also lost stock to the Indians and some were willing to help find them. Shortly thereafter, the combined force came upon and battled fifty or sixty Indians. Fairfield tells of the scene after the fight: "The two white men gathered up what bows and arrows they could find, the arrows all having stone points. Evidently the Indians had only one gun, for that was all the whites heard during the fight. They found 17 dead Indians and these they scalped and brought the scalps home with them."

When Bill Coombs Edwards, ran from Merced County he moved to Honey Lake, staying with Elliot and Gilpin. Sometime in April, about a month after Lucky Bill left the posse to warn

Edwards his whereabouts were suspected, Edwards moved. He went to live with another of the neversweats, John Mullen and his hired man, Asa Snow. Fairfield said: "Mullen had a few cattle and was said to be handy at picking up other people's calves."

When the Mormons had been preparing to leave Carson Valley in the fall of 1857 they sold a band of 100 Durham cows to two men from Honey Lake. The cattle were the finest ever brought to Honey Lake Valley. One of the men, a Frenchman of considerable means, took most of the cattle. The man's name was Henry Gordier. Chauncey Noteware reported that Gordier had a brother who was a ne'er-do-well: an alcoholic who sponged off him. In the spring of 1858 Gordier was known to have said that if he could sell his cattle he would leave the country and his brother would never find him. Noteware said: "Edwards then wrote to Thorington to dig up his money and put enough with it to buy Gordier's cattle and come up himself and they would buy the cattle. Thorington answered by saying that he did not have the money to do it."

Noteware's report continued: "Edwards and a man by the name Mullins conceived the idea of forging a bill of sale of the cattle and kill Gordier and as the latter had said he would secretly leave the country it would be thought that he had done so, after selling his cattle."

Sometime after Edwards went to live with Mullen the two men sought out Gordier. They told him he had a sick cow across the river, and offered to take him to it. "...they struck the river a little too high up and turned and went down it. They were riding side by side and Mullen dropped back a little and shot the Frenchman through the head..."

A month later when the murder was discovered, Edwards and Mullen disappeared (Mullen never to be seen again). Edwards would be tracked back to Carson Valley. He had again asked assistance from Lucky Bill. Word of Gordier's murder had carried to Carson Valley and Thorington confronted Edwards about it. Edwards swore to Lucky Bill that he had nothing to do with it. Lucky Bill again took Edwards at his word.

H.F. Dangberg, prominent settler, who feuded with Lucky Bill over land. Courtesy Nevada Historical Society.

Historian Myron Angel. After reading the trial transcript, he wrote that Thorington was guilty of nothing except trying to secure an outlaw's escape. Courtesy California Section, California State Library.

Historian Asa Merrill Fairfield. His account, based primarily on information from Honey Lake vigilantes, implied that Lucky Bill was guilty. Courtesy California Section, California State Library.

D.R. Hawkins was twelve years old at the time of Lucky Bill's hanging. He believed Thorington to be "a noble character." Courtesy Nevada Historical Society.

Above, Thorington's Genoa house, today. Below, pasture land below Thorington's Fredricksburg Ranch.

Henry Van Sickle was a leading citizen in Carson Valley. He said the whole Lucky Bill affair "had a suspicious odor." Drawing by Dorothy Makley.

A Miss Lamme, one of two daguerreotypes framed together. The other was of a gentleman named C. Hawkins. Could this have been Martha Lamb? Courtesy California Section, California State Library.

Emanuel "Manny" Penrod. Courtesy Nevada State Historical Society.

Orson Hyde. The Mormon leader who organized Carson Valley despite hostile opposition from members of The Committee. Courtesy Nevada Historical Society.

Captain William Weatherlow, leader of The Honey Lake Rangers (taken from a daguerreotype.) He turned back instead of riding to Carson Valley to arrest Lucky Bill. Courtesy California Section, California State Library.

Above, Lute Old's Cotton Hotel today. Below, Honey Lake Valley. Courtesy Nevada Historical Society.

Major William Ormsby, leader of The Committee, Thorington's bitter enemy. Courtesy Nevada Historical Society.

Numaga, leader of the Paiutes, a friend to Major Ormsby until the Paiute War of 1860. Courtesy Nevada Historical Society.

Elzy Knott, Lucky Bill's good friend. He helped organize the anti-vigilantes against The Committee. Courtesy Nevada Historical Society.

5

(22) i don't recolle ct of John Neal offering Lucey Bill the privolige ao selecting a jury. but but was given every show with in the reach of-ed justice. and Luckey Bill expressed himself satisfi with the jury, and expressed himself during the trial that his luck was gonen that the cards was stockedon him.

(23) i donot any Carson Valley joined any Honey L Lake people, only to do justice

(24) J.M.BALDWIN. RICHARD SIDES, and L,B,ABERNATHY

(25) i donot know of any men being arested in Honey Lake Valley and braught to Carson for trial, and i only lived three miles from Carson city, and in town most every day. if there was such an occurance , it is news to me,

the Cort that tried Kuckey Bill, was composed of JOHN CARY, Chief Justice. JOHN NEAL Associate justice

Gilpin as marshal or sherif. a jury was supenid in the regular way and examined as to qualificati by the Cort on one side ane the Prisoners on the other side. i donot that a fairer trial could be had,

hoping you may find the questions satisfactory

respectfully yours E, Penrod.

The last page of a letter from Manny Penrod to A.M. Fairfield dated July 22, 1912. Courtesy California Section, California State Library.

This barn is on the site at the Clear Creek Ranch where Lucky Bill's trial was held. It may or may not be the original structure. Photo by permission of Donald and Kate Schulz.

Chauncey N. Noteware, who became the Secretary of State of Nevada. He took down the trial testimony at the request of Lucky Bill, who told Noteware he was certain to be executed. Courtesy Nevada Historical Society.

Carson Valley pioneers. Seated second from left is member of The Committee Walter Cosser who was barred from participation in the hanging of Edwards. Next to Cosser on the end is Thorington's co-defendant, reputed Boarder Ruffian, Lute Olds. Standing, second from right, is juror Manny Penrod. Courtesy Nevada Historical Society.

Chapter Nine

THE VIGILANTES ACT

Mullen's hired hand Snow had moved into Gordier's cabin. Mullen and Edwards were telling neighbors that Gordier had sold out, met a friend and left for France. Gordier's alcoholic brother contacted some of the neversweats. He insisted that Gordier would never have left without telling him.

A time later the company that had killed the Indians near Goose Lake returned to Honey Lake. Fairfield said: "The Goose Lake party got home not far from the first of May, and as this was the only diversion to be had in the country, the boys thought they must have a dance to celebrate the event. There were the three Mormon women [from the wagon train] and they managed to get three or four more and had their dance..." Having so few women at a dance allowed abundant time for talk: the main topic being the sudden departure of Gordier. The day after the dance one of the neversweats took Edwards aside, telling him something was not right in the Frenchman's disappearance and that many of the boys believed the incident required further investigation. Edwards and Mullen left Honey Lake that day. Their flight incited even stronger suspicions.

Sometime earlier men camping near the Susan River had heard an unaccountable gunshot and seen a fire. It was said that they now came forward suggesting the area be searched. A Mrs. Coulthurst, the wife of Gordier's ex-partner, later said that, "...she dreamed where the Frenchman's body was and told the men to look there for it." Whether occasioned by common or uncommon perception several Honey Lakers now investigated the site of a fire near the river. There, they found charred metal buttons, as if clothing had been burned, and dried blood which when analyzed, was adjudged human. Using a hook on a pole in a nearby hole in the river the men soon produced the decomposing body tied around a rock.

The chief suspects, Edwards and Mullen, were gone but others were still in the area. The neversweats focused first on Rough Elliot and his partner, Gilpin. These men knew the accused well, having housed one. When confronted they admitted knowing that Edwards' name was not Coombs and it was he who had killed Snelling in Merced County (in self-defense), but they denied knowledge of the immediate crime. It was suggested that they could be cleared of suspicion if they assisted in investigating the case. Elliot left immediately to begin an investigation in Carson Valley. Gilpin would follow in a few days. A man named John Neale and two others who had taken an interest stayed behind to pursue the case at Honey Lake. It was mid-May.

On Thursday, June 10th, 1858 the San Francisco *Daily Alta* ran a small announcement at the bottom of a column that preceeded its advertising section:

> HANGING IN HONEY LAKE VALLEY.—*We are indebted to Mr. Whiting, of Whiting's Express, for the information that a man named Snow was hung in Honey Lake Valley Monday last, by the citizens. He confessed having been accessory to the murder of the Frenchman, some weeks since, in the valley. He implicates two other men, now supposed to be in the lower country.* — Marysville News.

This report illustrates one role of the era's press, spreading information intended to justify a deed after the fact. Snow had, indeed, been hung. But, he had confessed nothing nor implicated anyone. He had not been an accessory. The Honey Lake Sheriff, Orlando Streshly, reported that Edwards later told him: "There was no one present but Mullen and I when we killed him [Gordier] and we would not trust Snow with a secret." Fairfield said: "He [Snow] denied knowing anything about the murder of Gordier." Accounts of those at Snow's hanging disagree on many points, but none said that Snow confessed anything.

Fairfield's compilation of information from those present led him to write this version: "John Neale and a crowd from the upper end of the valley went down to the Breed cabin. Probably they were joined by others as they went along and also by men living in that vicinity. There may have been a sort of trial or investigation that lasted into the night. Snow insisted that he was innocent and was very abusive and defiant and finally dared them to hang him. About two thirds of a mile south of east of the cabin and a quarter of a mile from the lake there were two pine trees. The larger tree, the one farthest from the lake, had a large limb growing at almost a right angle with the trunk and twelve or fifteen feet from the ground, and to this tree they went taking Snow with them. They intended to show him what hanging was like and probably thought they could scare him into making a confession. They pulled him up and let him hang awhile and then let him down and questioned him. He said he knew nothing to tell and cursed and defied them. They pulled him up again, let him down and questioned him, and the result was the same. He was pulled up the third time and this time they let him hang too long - when they let him down he was dead."

R. W. Young, who lived near Honey Lake Valley at the time, allows a different slant in his view of the hanging and the victim. He said that Snow was a very delicate man, far gone with consumption. There had been no evidence against him, said Young, except a rope under his bunk: "some considered [the rope] looked suspicious and afterward masked themselves and took poor Snow in the dead of night and hanged him I always thot they murdered poor Snow."

In May word had carried to Carson Valley that Gordier was missing and that it was suspected he had been murdered by Edwards and Mullen. Edwards and Mullen had separated, with Edwards taking Mullen's horse, Bald Hornet. Mullen apparently thought the horse a liability for it was a thousand pound, bald-faced chestnut sorrel; a racehorse known up and down the Sierras. Edwards rode Bald Hornet to the mountains above Genoa, secretly seeking out Lucky Bill.

Chauncey Noteware wrote the following account of occurrences at this juncture: "...suspicion then pointed to Edwards — Mullins in the meantime having left the country — whereupon Edwards secretly left the Valley and came to Thorington in Carson Valley, with the intention of getting the money left with Thorington, sell a valuable horse and with the proceeds go to South America.

"In the mean time the news of the murder of Gordier had reached Carson Valley & when Edwards asked for his money Thorington said to him, 'Edwards if you had any hand in killing Gordier, and palming yourself on me, you are the most ungrateful wretch alive! Edwards answered him that he had no part in the killing of Gordier...'"

Even with Edwards denial, Thorington was reluctant to allow Edwards to stay around him. At the trial Edwards said that Lucky Bill told him that he had befriended him once when in trouble but now thought it best that he "get out of the way, go over the mountains, etc." Part of Thorington's hesitancy to help stemmed from the fact that some Honey Lakers had been seeking Edwards and had now discovered Coombs and Edwards were the same man. Knowing Lucky Bill to have been his friend, they realized the gambler had helped him evade them all these months.

Rumor had it that the Honey Lakers now not only wanted to settle-up with Edwards, but also with his accomplice, Lucky Bill. At the trial Richard N. Allen, the attorney known as Tennessee, said: "Thorington has told me on many occasions that he was willing to go before a legal tribunal and be tried; I have heard from Thorington and Peter Vallely that the people of Honey Lake Valley had collected, and were in the vicinity for the purpose of arresting Thorington, and taking him to Honey Lake Valley, and hanging him without judge or jury, and I believed it at the time." Peter Vallely said: "I got the report of the rising of the citizens of Honey Lake from Thorington himself; he did not say from whom he got his information."

Despite his qualms, Lucky Bill helped Edwards. The day after meeting with him, Thorington sent his son Jerome to Merced to collect a debt owed to Edwards. He also had Jerome ride to Marysville to alert Mullen of the excitement at Honey Lake. Jerome collected $350 and a mare in partial payment of the debt owed Edwards ($600 more was owed), but never made contact with Mullen.

Edwards testified that after his meeting with Lucky Bill, he stayed in the mountains. He came down once or twice at night to Lute Olds' hotel where he purchased food on credit; this, after "making himself known" to the hotel keeper (he had heretofore known Olds "but slightly"). Once, outside Olds' place Edwards met with Lucky Bill so he could get the money Jerome brought from Merced. Jerome Thorington testified that Edwards planned to go either to Salt Lake City or Valpariso. One of Olds' hands, Cal Austin, who Jerome said, was known to have been "run off the East Fork for stealing horses in California," intended to accompany Edwards if he went to Salt Lake but did not have enough money if he chose to go to Valpariso.

When Rough Elliot arrived in Carson Valley, he received a cool reception. People believed he had come to try to arrest Lucky Bill and take him back to Honey Lake. The third night after his arrival a friend of Lucky Bill's approached him. At the trial Elliot reported: "McBride told me that if my business was to arrest Thorington, he was willing to give himself up to any civil authority, as he did not believe they could prove enough against him to convict him of anything criminal in any Court of Justice; that Thorington was willing to be tried by the citizens of Carson Valley, but would not go to Honey Lake Valley; I then tried by every endeavor to convince McBride that my intentions towards Thorington were of the most friendly nature, and by this means obtained an interview with him."

Rough Elliot was finally taken to Thorington's house. During their meeting Thorington told Elliot he believed Edwards was innocent. At the trial Elliot said: "Thorington told me he did not believe that Edwards was guilty of the murder of Gordier; he appeared at the time to have but little confidence in me."

Shortly after this meeting Junius Brutus Gilpin arrived in Genoa with a plan to entrap Thorington. At the trial Gilpin said: "I tried to gain his confidence through pretense of having stolen a horse from Honey Lake Valley; I claimed his protection; in this I failed in a great measure; I had hurt my mare, or the one I was riding, and Thorington offered me fifty dollars to pay the damages and settle the difficulty, and to return the mare to Mr. Johnson to whom she belongs; Thorington would never tell me where Edwards was, but said he was over the mountain."

Elliot's insistance that he wished to help their friend finally won Lucky Bill over. Thorington took Elliot to meet with Bill Edwards.

The three men met at the ford of a slough near Mott's field, holding a rambling conversation that spanned several hours. Edwards commented "there was something said of almost everything". One of the topics was raising money to get Edwards out of the country.

Rough Elliot told of a scheme proposed by him, wherein he and Gilpin would pretend to have a gun battle with Edwards and capture Bald Hornet while Edwards escaped. Then they would sell the horse, and secure the money for Edwards. It was mentioned that perhaps a third party should accompany the two Honey Lakers to act as a witness. Elliot said: "Thorington then suggested that Barber be this third person, as it was well known that he was an enemy of his, and would give good color to the transaction and free him, Thorington, from all suspicion in the transaction." The conversation then turned — there would be danger to Edwards if Barber got too close to him. Edwards assured the others that if Barber got too close he (Edwards) would kill him. Lucky Bill then commented that if someone was to be killed he would prefer it be either Richard Sides or Major Ormsby; he would, he added, pay good money to have Ormsby killed. Elliot suggested that it wouldn't do to create any more difficulty. Lucky Bill agreed and they concluded that Barber should be the one to go along.

94 The Hanging of Lucky Bill

Because we don't have Lucky Bill's version of this conversation, it is impossible to know the tone of his comment. Could it have been said in jest or idly, in passing? Regardless, the statement was to become the source of rumors spread in newspapers about Lucky Bill trying to assassinate Ormsby.

Because of a mixup, the plan was carried out in somewhat different fashion than was discussed. Jerome Thorington was involved as the third man instead of Barber. Snowshoe Thompson reported to the Sacramento *Union* from Genoa on June 14th: "The notorious Bill Edwards who murdered Snelling has been around here the last four days, and has been pursued by a number of persons. Yesterday they found him on the trail above Daggett's and captured his horse. They shot six or eight times at Edwards, he returning their fire twice. He fled to the mountains and got away. His horse proved to be the celebrated racehorse 'Bald Hornet'."

The plan to sell Edwards' horse would not be carried out. Rough Elliot had been keeping Major Ormsby apprised of the situation. Word had been sent to the neversweats. The morning after Thompson's report left the valley thirty riders from Honey Lake, joined by some from Washoe Valley had arrived in Genoa. There, they joined forces with Major Ormsby and The Committee.

Chapter Ten

THE ARRESTS AND TRIAL

Within twenty-four hours of receiving word that Edwards was in Carson Valley, thirty-two Honey Lakers were ready to ride. Fairfield listed those who went: John H. Neale, Cap Hill, William Weatherlow, U. J. Tutt, William Dow, Fred Hines, Henry Arnold, D. M. Munchie, Thad Norton, Richard Thompson, Anotone Storff, Tom. McMurtry, John C. Davis, "Mormon Joe" Owens, John Mote, _____ Henderson, William N. Crawford, William H. Clark, A. G. Epstein, Frank Johnson, William Meyers, R. W. Young, _____ Hughes, Alec Chapman, George Lathrop, Thomas J.Harvey, Thomas Watson, John Baxter, Mark Haviland, _____McVeagh, Mat. Craft and R.J. Scott.

Cap. Hill, whose real name was William Hill Naileigh, was, at times, a leader in Honey Lake Valley. He was on the committee to form a government that met in Genoa in 1857 and later, when they mustered a Civil War force in the area was named First Lieutnant (he was the only one from this list named among fourteen officers). But, Fairfield said: "There is a possibility that instead of Hill another man went, but it is impossible to tell who it was." This points up the fact that Honey Lake's leaders did not make the trip. Neither Issac Roop nor Peter Lassen rode with the band. William Weatherlow, the leader of the Honey Lake Rangers, started out but "got sick" and with the man named McVeagh turned back after one night's ride. Neither Orlando Streshly, the Honey Lake Sheriff, nor Solomon Perrin, the ex-Carson Valley lawyer who served at least once as an arbitrator in a Honey Lake land dispute, participated. This, even though conversations between Perrin and Thorington were crucial to the prosecution's case and were given by another of the neversweats as he thought they had occurred.

The Honey Lakers who rode into Carson Valley were men of action, used to violence. U.J. Tutt was one of Weatherlow's lieutenants. Fairfield described how earlier in the year fighting Indians, Tutt helped when Weatherlow was engaged in hand to

96   The Hanging of Lucky Bill

hand combat: "He [Tutt] ran up and caught the Indian by the hair and with one stroke of his bowie knife almost cut off his head." Dow and several others were also Indian fighters. Alec. Chapman was the man who nearly fought Rough Elliot on the Goose Lake expedition. A month later, in July, one of the riders, Mat. Craft, would kill another, R. J. Scott.

To avoid detection the men rode by night, camping in wooded areas during the day. As they came closer to Genoa other men joined them. Fairfield said: "In Washoe Valley they were joined by a few men, probably Masons who knew of their coming." Fairfield also says the men who joined the gang in Genoa were Masons. The murdered Snelling had been a Mason and the organization had offered a large reward for his killer. However, Thorington's trial was not a plot by Masons. C. N. Noteware was a leading Mason — a Senior Deacon and later Grand Secretary. It was he who recorded and published the transcript of the trial and years later, on Masonic stationary, wrote to Fairfield recounting its injustices. One of the men who joined the Honey Lakers was Theodore Winters, a relative newcomer to Washoe Valley; a burly, walrus-mustachioed man who would carve out a niche in Nevada's early ranching and horse racing history.

The riders reached Genoa on Monday, June 14th, just before daybreak. Rough Elliot met them and they tied their horses behind a long barn at the edge of Main Street. Major Ormsby and others from The Committee joined them. "Major Ormsby told them afterwards that he and his wife sat up all night."

Elliot took charge, directing men into position.

By Wednesday, June 17th, the report on the front page of the San Francisco *Daily Alta* (the same as appeared in the Sacramento *Union* on the same day) included the following: "On Monday morning last before daylight a body of armed horsemen, numbering about 100 men, charged into Carson Valley, and took possession of all the roads and trails leading from the valley into the mountains...

"All egress was cut off from the valley by a strong armed guard, and those wishing to pass out or into the valley are furnished with passports..."

Once the roads were secure Elliot led most of the men to Lucky Bill's house. They surrounded it and as the sun rose Theodore Winters went in. He first brought out Lucky Bill, then Jerome. Maria Thorington followed, pleading for her boy, "but," reported R. W. Young; "not a word for her husband."

A group went to a hotel, presumably Lucky Bill's White House, and placed his friends' Orin Gray and John McBride in custody. All prisoners were then taken to an upstairs room in The Singleton Hotel (T.J. Singleton would give testimony at the trial and later became the second of three husbands to Mrs. Haines at whose house the vigilantes usually met). The prisoners were kept under guard while the vigilantes ate breakfast.

Outside the hotel the streets were charged. Many years later D. R. Hawkins recounted: "At the age of twelve, in 1858 in Genoa, Nevada I arose early one bright morning in June to find the town thronged with armed men who styled themselves a vigilance committee and soon learned that they had taken into custody Wm. B. Thorington — popularly known as 'Lucky Bill,' and that they were after one Bill Edwards a supposed murderer.

"In company with my father and by permission of the guards I went upstairs in the Singleton hotel and saw there at the far corner of the large room Lucky Bill, bound and reclining on the floor. As we approached him my father said, 'Well Bill, what is all this about?' and he replied, 'Mr. Hawkins, these men have come here to hang me and I guess they are going to do it.'"

After breakfasting, Rough Elliot led a group out to Lute Olds' Cotton Hotel where they arrested Olds, his brother-in-law — Ike Gandy, and Calvin Austin. Gandy started to fight but was subdued by Elliot brandishing his pistol.

In the afternoon the seven prisoners were taken from town. Fairfield says: "...that afternoon the Neversweats and their prisoners, accompanied by a few of the Carson country settlers, went down the river to the Clear Creek ranch then owned by R. D. Sides, L. B. Abernathy, and J. M. Baldwin."

The ranch was removed from Lucky Bill's friends in Genoa. It was a station with a large barn where many men and horses could gather. It also was bounded by flat, treeless land assuring the vigilantes that they could not be surprised by Thorington supporters. Plans to arrest Bill Edwards were now made. Travel in and out of the valley was controlled, as were communications. Influenced by emotions, rumors and lies spread.

The report of June 17, 1858 that appeared in the San Francisco *Daily Alta* and The Sacramento *Union* stated:

> ...but it appears that Snow turned State's evidence on the scaffold, confessing that he belonged to a regular band of thieves, and gave signs, & etc., by which one member could recognize another of the gang, and gave the names of several parties living in Carson Valley who were concerned in the murder of the Frenchman. It was given out that Snow

98 The Hanging of Lucky Bill

was duly executed, and the matter kept quiet. Two men were dispatched to Carson Valley, where they have been for a month, initiating themselves into the good graces of the band, finding out their secrets, &c., by the signs given them by Snow.

The report went on to list those arrested:

W.B. Thornton, alias 'Lucky Bill;' his son, Jerome Thornton, aged about 17 years; Luther Olds, Orrin Gray, McWade, a gambler, and two men in the employ of Olds known as Little Ike and Colonel.

The "news" story concluded:

It is reported that a scheme was laid for the assassination of Major W. M. Ormsby early on Monday morning by the gang of desperadoes. The Major has been active in aiding to ferret out the parties. It was arranged to waylay him on his route to Placerville, where he proposed going that morning.

Edwards, who committed a murder at Snelling's ranch, on the San Juaquin river, last fall, is said to be the party detailed to silence the Major on Daggit's trail, leading out of the valley, but the timely arrival of the party from Honey Lake detained him, and perhaps saved his life.

Newspapers which had little control over communiques from Utah Territory to begin with, now had none. In the emotionally charged atmosphere, unconfirmed "reports" were rapidly disseminated and distorted. In its June 18th edition the *Herald* added erroneous detail to the *Alta* report:

On Monday last, a party of about one hundred men arrived in Carson Valley from Honey Lake, in search of the murderers of the Frenchman, who was murdered at Honey Lake some time since. These men report that they arrested at Honey Lake a man by the name of Snow, whom they suspected of having had something to do with the murder. By means of threats, and by hanging him up for a time they forced him to confess the whole matter and disclose the names of his accomplices. Snow told them when and where the murder was committed, and that they had thrown the body loaded with stones into a stream near Honey Lake. The party then made search, and found the body as represented by Snow. He told them that there was an organized band on that side of the mountain whose objects were to rob steal, and murder, and that most of said band reside in Carson Valley. He further said that the members of the band had signs, pass-words and grips by which to recognize each other, and informed them what the signs, pass-words and grips were.

This report also incorrectly stated: "Some others are said to be in custody at Honey Lake." It concluded with another purported threat to Major Ormsby: "Major Ormsby has taken an active part in ferreting out this matter, and it is reported that Lucky Bill has offered a reward of fifty head of cattle to any one who will kill him."

Also, on the 18th the Sacramento *Daily Bee* joined in circulating untruths: "We learn from a telegram in the *Statesmen* and *Union* of this morning, that the story about the hanging of Snow was a ruse which the people of Honey Lake Valley adopted to capture a whole band of thieves. Snow it appears, turned State's evidence; said that he was one of a regular gang of robbers several of whom were in Carson Valley..." It continued with the regular line that there were secret signs used by two Honey Lakers to gain the confidence of the gang, that 100 men had taken control of Carson Valley, that seven citizens had been arrested ("They were placed under strong guard to await a hearing before Judge Lynch, and a People's Jury" — it said), and that a scheme to assassinate Major Ormsby had been averted by the arrival of the Honey Lakers. In the article a Mr. Alden is quoted as saying: "The inhabitants of the valleys breathe freer at present than they have done for two years knowing that there was an organized band of robbers and murderers amongst them and that as they have now got the leaders in their hands it will be a means of breaking up the organization."

There is no listing or mention of a Mr. Alden residing in the territory. Moreover, his comment is contradicted by prominent Carson Valley citizens: Henry Van Sickle, Chauncey Noteware, and D. R. Hawkins (who said only four men in all Carson Valley were glad of Thorington's arrest and that all four had had business differences with him). Another Genoa resident, D. H. Holdridge, commented that he did not even know the names of anyone who participated with the Honey Lakers and that, in fact: "very few went in with the Honey Lakers in capturing and trying Lucky Bill." In 1882 historians Fariss and Smith said: "The majority of the old residents of Carson and Eagle Valleys, where he [Lucky Bill] resided are firmly convinced of his innocence."

The other untruths, specifically that Snow testified that he was part of a gang and that there was a gang at all were disproved by testimony at the trial and the subsequent statements of those involved. The rumor that Ormsby was fingered for assassination almost certainly sprang from Rough Elliot's account of the plan to secure Bald Hornet (when Lucky Bill commented that if anyone was to be killed he would prefer it be Sides or Ormsby). The suggestion that Edwards would be in a position to ambush Ormsby was highly improbable since Edwards was on the run and heavily sought after. Communication in and out of the valley was controlled by the vigilantes and it may be surmised that the persons transmitting the misinformation were attempting to lay groundwork for what was to come.

Jerome Thorington was used to bait Edwards into being captured. R. W. Young said: "They told Jerome Thornton they would give him his liberty if he would go out to woods and bring in Edwards or Combs as he called himself. Jerome said if he was guilty of any wrong that he would suffer the penalty but that he would not betray a friend. his Father beged him to go saying that Edwards Evidence would clear him."

Fairfield said: "It has been told that they promised to let Lucky Bill go, too, but the Honey Lake men say they made no such promise. It is said that Jerome didn't want to betray Edwards; but his father told him that Edwards testimony would clear him and finally the boy agreed to do what they wanted him to."

Just before dark Jerome left for the hills to find Edwards. At the same time Elliot, Gilpin, Dow, Theodore Winters and eight others departed for Lucky Bill's river ranch where Martha Lamb and her baby lived.

Jerome brought Edwards to the ranch. As they entered the house two men with clubs hit Edwards. A shotgun he carried before him received the impact of one blow, breaking both barrels from the stock. The other blow landed on his head. He was tied and bandaged and William Dow reported: "...the first words Edwards spoke were 'I deserve it.'" Dow's memory, here, may have been colored by the wishfullnes of age. Closer to expectations of what the killer might have said was the quote in the San Francisco *Herald* of June 19th:

Edwards said he only wished to live to kill five men, viz: Maj. Ormsby. R. Sides, Wade, Buckner and J.L. Carry, prominent citizens, and who had taken active part in breaking up and arresting the band.

The men stayed at the ranch that night. The next morning Edwards, unnoticed, managed to get free of his leg bindings and run. He was caught by Elliot just as he jumped into a nearby slough. Back in Genoa, Edwards was placed in irons for the trip to Clear Creek Ranch. "Joseph Frey says that the blacksmith's name was G. W. Hepperly and that the irons, one of them made from the handle of an old frying-pan, were riveted on and a chain put between them."

While Edwards was being made secure Rough Elliot gathered a crowd with his tale of the capture, escape and recapture. D. R. Hawkins said: "I saw Elliot at that time take from his pockets and exhibit two purses of gold which I understood he had taken from Edwards at the time of the capture. One of the purses was nearly as large as a Bologna sausage."

Fairfield noted that few of Lucky Bill's friends made the ride out to Clear Creek Ranch. The other anti-vigilantes were in hiding. They feared that whatever was to happen to Thorington might also happen to them.

The first night an excitement at Clear Creek roused the vigilantes. A report circulated that Uncle Billy Rogers had gathered 100 men and was coming to rescue Lucky Bill. The prisoners were locked inside rooms in Sides' ranch house. Guards kept watch through the night. The rescuers did not show; the report had been the consequence of rattled nerves; Uncle Billy was still far across the Sierras.

The trial was held in the barn. Carson Valley's John Cary served as judge; John Neale of Honey Lake and Dr. King of Eagle Valley were associates. Rough Elliot acted as sheriff, J. B. Gilpin as deputy. "A jury of 18 of the vigilantes was called 12 of the number to find a verdict." A list of jurors was never compiled. By their own statements, William Dow served, as did Manny Penrod and Joseph Frey — an eight month resident of Genoa. The other fifteen, though the object of much speculation, have never been positively identified. When asked, D. R. Hawkins responded merely: "They were selected from the mob."

Chauncey Noteware took down the testimony. Noteware said that Edwards was not put on trial: "They were tried by the committee at the Clear Creek ranch, having first secured the arrest of Edwards, who was their own witness in the trial of 'Lucky Bill.' Edwards himself — not being on trial — convicted on his own confession."

On June 18 the Sacramento *Union* reported: "The cases were being tried secretly; hence nothing is known outside the jury room." Any spectators allowed inside the barn must have been friendly to the vigilantes, for historians Fariss and Smith commented: "The judges, jurors and spectators sat in the courtroom, armed with guns and revolvers."

The secrecy gave further impetus to speculation. The same day the Sacramento *Daily Bee* concluded their rumor-filled account: "Mr. Childs says, that Lucky Bill, L. Olds, and Edwards will certainly be hung, and that the rest will probably be banished, except Jerome Thornton, who, owing to his youth, and doubtless being under fear of his father, has been compelled to participate in their crimes."

As for the trial itself, Orin Gray, McBride and Ike Gandy (whom newspapers called "Little Ike") were each acquitted — there being no evidence against them. T. J. Singleton, at whose hotel the accused had first been held, testified that a man named Bannen told him that he feared there was a plan to rob or injure him [Bannen] the previous September. Bannen suspected that McBride, the hotel manager — D. E. Gilbert, and a man named Hawes were involved: "...he said it might be conjecture in him, but he had been in the habit through life of watching men, and if they made a false step he was apt to detect it; and that three moves had been made that night which aroused his suspicion — one, the losing of the watch, which was to be the means of getting him out of doors; another, McBride did not, as was his custom, lock the door upon going to bed; the other movement I don't remember." The jurors apparently felt there was more conjecture than detection in this heresay and it was summarily dismissed. This seems to have been the extent of testimony about gang behavior at the trial. The "gang" of the news reports had proven non-existant.

Owing to his youth, Jerome Thorington was also released, although he admitted helping his father help Edwards. Lute Olds was found guilty of assisting Edwards — "harboring a fugitive" according to the *Daily Alta*. Olds was fined $875 and banished from the country under penalty of being shot. Calvin Austin was similarly banished, being fined $220; he had not actually assisted Edwards, but had planned to travel with him when he left. These cases being resolved left only the fate of Lucky Bill to be considered.

Neither Lucky Bill's testimony, if in fact it was taken, nor any of the defendants statements (except Jerome Thorington's) still exists. What has survived is a transcript written by Chauncey Noteware recording the testimony of ten witnesses: L. M. Breed, William Edwards, B. Cherry, T. J. Atchison, Jerome Thorington, T. W. C. Elliot, J. B. Gilpin, T. J. Singleton, Richard Allen and P. Vallely.

Myron Angel who read Noteware's entire transcription some years after the incident said: "The evidence under oath was written down by C. N. Noteware, late Secretary of State of Nevada; and the writer of this has read it all. Not a thing appears there implicating Lucky Bill in anything except the attempt to secure the murderer's escape. The absence of any knowledge on the part of the accused of the guilt of Edwards, is a noticeable feature in that testimony; that party, after having aknowledged his own guilt, swore positively that he had assured Lucky Bill that he was innocent, and no one else testified to the contrary."

Edwards' exact testimony concerning Lucky Bill's knowledge of the crime was: "Thorington had no knowledge of the murder of Gordier, that I know of; I had no conversation with Thorington concerning the murder, previous to the death of Gordier; he made no arrangement with me in regard to purchasing Gordier's stock when he visited Honey Lake; he told me his business was hunting horse thieves and murderers, and that he came to my house to borrow money on which to return to Carson Valley..." Later in his testimony, while telling of Lucky Bill sending Jerome to Merced County to try to collect money owed him, Edwards said: "At the time Jerome was sent I denied to Thorington the murder of Gordier."

Rough Elliot, the prosecution's other leading witness, corroborated Edwards' statements in his testimony: "Thorington told me he did not believe that Edwards was guilty of the murder of Gordier." In the extant testimony no other witness addresses the issue.

L. M. Breed, from Honey Lake (the mob had met at Breed's cabin to interrogate Snow before hanging him), raised the issue that seems to have been taken to insinuate guilt on Thorington's part. "L. M. Breed, sworn. — Reside in Honey Lake Valley, about a half mile from McMurtry & Perrin's. Two or three weeks previous to the murder of Henry Gordier, W. O. Thorington arrived in Honey Lake Valley. He called at the residence of McMurtry & Perrin, and wanted to procure an animal to go and see Henry Gordier's cattle; he thought of buying them; he got an animal and went away; on his return he offered to pay for the use of the animal, remarking that he had no money when he procured it, but that he had seen Coombs since he had been gone, and obtained money, and now had plenty; McMurtry or Perrin asked him if he bought Harry Gordier's stock; he said no, but that he had made arrangements with Coombs to purchase them."

The insinuation taken from Breed's testimony was that at his meeting with Edwards, Thorington conspired to murder Gordier. It is strange that this evidence was not even substantiated by one of the principals. Perrin was not at the trial; McMurtry does not seem to have been called as a witness. This hearsay appears to be the entire evidence used to convict Lucky Bill of being an accomplice to murder.

B. Cherry testified that when they were together on the posse Thorington mentioned he would like to go to Honey Lake and see the Frenchman's stock. But, when they learned that the men they were chasing had gone to Honey Lake, no further mention of Gordier was made. Instead, when the opportunity arose, Thorington left the others so he might "get money to buy supplies to get back to Carson Valley." He then rode to see Edwards. He conducted two items of business when he encountered Edwards: borrowed $15 and gave Edwards a letter saying his where-abouts were suspected by those chasing him. Did Thorington also discuss Gordier's cattle, or was that merely a ruse he had planned to use once he was close to Honey Lake in order to contact and warn Edwards?

Neither this nor any other possible explanation of Thorington's motive seems to have been explored at the trial. The innuendo that Lucky Bill had met Edwards in order to plan the murder of Gordier was allowed to stand, though it was contradicted by Edwards' testimony.

A. M. Fairfield apparently did not have access to Noteware's trial transcript. In his book he used William Dow's recounting of trial testimony: "Dow says Edwards testified that while Lucky Bill was in Honey Lake valley he helped plan the murder of the Frenchman." Because Edward's testimony still exists we know this statement to be directly opposed to the truth. William Dow was one of the jurors.

Chapter Eleven

THE EXECUTION

Jury member Emanual Penrod later claimed that the action taken against Lucky Bill was not a vigilante action, but a fair trial. Using his singular style, Penrod wrote: "The actions of this Court has been Called in all the Historys and writings of Nevada a Vigelants Comity, formed untel after these hangings, when there was a Comity Organised, but never had any work to do.
"i must say in the work of bringing to Justises there Murderers, Rufe Elliott Did some of the best Detective work ever done; what ever Rufe was after this, he did a sharp piece of Detective work in this....His enemys always accused him of taking underhanded means in his Detective work, but I think any detective would have done as he did. He brought to light a murder for gain in which a Rancher who thought he was selling for cash, when his life was the price. i wright this only to show that the Hanging was not by a Vigalance Comitty as has been reported." In a letter to A. M. Fairfield, Penrod also said: "am familiar with trial and execution of Wm, Thornton (Luckey Bill. as i was one of the jury who tried him, and so heared all the evidence.and i must say that he (Luckey Bill) had as fair a Trial as any one-ever had." The evidence does not support Penrod's contentions. In no reasonable trial would hearsay and innuendo, contradicted by sworn testimony, be evidence to hang a man.

The assertion that Thorington was the leader of a gang had been disproven. In fact, no evidence was produced to suggest the existance of a gang. The only crime of which Thorington was guilty was the same for which Lute Olds was convicted — "harboring a fugitive."

But, no amount of evidence was going to outweigh Lucky Bill's other offenses. He was a gambler, who promoted individualism instead of civil obedience. His business concerns had created enemies. In assisting Edwards he had stood against the Masons. In his dealings with the Mormons he had stood against members of The Committee. He had two wives. There was testimony that

106   The Hanging of Lucky Bill

he had suggested killing Sides or Ormsby. The sentence was death by hanging.

Throughout the months before Thorington's arrest members of The Committee had sought to topple Lucky Bill. After the trial, Carson Valley citizens pointed accusingly at Ormsby as the ringleader. On June 21st a letter defending Major Ormsby was sent to the Placerville *Mountain Democrat* by a man calling himself "Jerry." In it he professed to tell what had occurred at the trial, then said: "Now I wish to say something in relation to the predjudice and excitement sought to be created against Major Wm. M. Ormsby. Thorington and some of his friends have endeavored and in fact have made some people believe, that Major Ormsby has been the sole cause of all the excitement, because Thorington and Major O. were enemies, and Major had influence &c....In the first place I know Ormsby had nothing to do or say in this affair, only in searching out crime and bringing the guilty to trial...

"...It was proved that Thorington had engaged in a plot to murder Mr. Barber, and 'that he would give — (the amount not remembered) dollars to have Major Ormsby killed or Richard Sides, it made no particular difference which or both, that they were enemies of his, Thorington's.' Who can blame Major O. for wanting to see Thorington properly punished?

"I have now, gentlemen, given you merely an idea of the affair; and before I close I will say the verdict rendered against 'Lucky Bill' well known in your city, was severe and terrible — but what better could the people of this valley do?..."

Reviewing statements about the trial it becomes apparent that emotional contagion, rather than justice, brought about the "severe and terrible" sentence. Thorington's fate had been decided before the jury voted. Several witnesses report the same thing: the building of Lucky Bill's gallows took place before the verdict was returned. "The jury was out sometime, occupying a room in the upper story of the Clear Creek ranch building. During their deliberations they sent for Mr. Noteware to read them certain portions of the evidence. While so reading he heard noise of carpenter work. He looked out of the window and saw the cross beam — or gallows being made for the hanging of 'Lucky Bill.'"

Unfounded rumors and false statements continued to appear in the papers: On June 22nd the Sacramento *Daily Union* reported that Crandall's stage had carried news that Thorington had a bill of sale for Gordier's cattle (which would have been evidence of a deal between Edwards and Thorington); and, on July 3rd "Jerry" wrote to the Placerville *Mountain Democrat* saying that it had been proved there was a gang of thieves and harborers of murderers in Carson Valley and that evidence had been taken down which would prove Thorington's guilt. Neither the bill of sale nor Jerry's evidence was ever produced. And, Noteware's record of the trial testimony contradicted these statements.

On Saturday morning June 19th Lucky Bill Thorington was brought shackled from the barn, guarded by J. M. Baldwin and A. P. Squires. Fairfield reports that R. W. Young watched an exchange between Rough Elliot and Jerome Thorington: "Young says that just before Lucky Bill was taken away to be executed Elliot went up to Jerome, standing near-by, and offered him his hand saying 'I'll bid you goodby.' The boy threw back his hand and said he would never shake hands with any man who helped murder his father." Young also reported that Lucky Bill said "a cool fairwell" to Maria and "made a great racket with his chains" when Martha Lamb arrived. "When the time came they placed him in a wagon with armed guards on Either side and drove to the gallows which was Erected for this purpose while the trial was in progress. before he was hanged he told some friend present to tell Billy Rogers that if he had been here this would not have happened."

There are several versions of Lucky Bill's last moments; all agree that he was composed. It is said that he met death cooly: tossing away his necktie and replacing it with the rope, saying: "If they want to hang me, I'm no hog;" that he met death easily, singing "The Last Rose of Summer;" and, that he died boldly, swinging himself out of the wagon before it drove away.

Young Lawrence Frey, the teenage son of one of the jurors, was the driver of the wagon. Elzyette Knott Selby said he was haunted all his life by the act and that he had been tricked into it. "...they drew straws to see who'd do the hanging. They played a trick on him alright....The one who drew the short straw had to drive the mules and because he was a kid the older ones arranged that he was the one to draw it."

Grace Dangberg focused her account of the execution on the young teamster: "The 'Committee', all young men in their twenties and thirties, who hanged their prisoner on that regrettable day in July 1858, forced the protesting Lawrence to mount the wagon on which 'Lucky Bill' stood in the shadows of the gallows and to take in his hands the reins of the team of mules. When the weeping teenager hesitated, 'Lucky Bill' came to the rescue with his unfailing gallantry: 'Drive out, Boy,' he said."

Chapter Twelve

FATES OF THE PRINCIPALS

"...[Anti-viglantes] took Lucky Bill down from where he was hanging on Averill Hill, secreted him away and buried him twenty odd miles away on his own ranch at night."

The next morning, Sunday, June 20th, the men from Honey Lake left Genoa. In their midst the murderer Bill Edwards rode Bald Hornet. Fairfield reported: "He [Edwards] was not tied, and all the way home he rode along and talked just the same as the others. T. and W. [Thompson and West, *History of Nevada*] say that Theodore Winters, Walter Cosser, and Samuel Swager were appointed a committee to go to Honey Lake and see that Edwards was hanged, but the Honey Lakers say they never came along with them."

Because there were no first hand witnesses from Carson Valley many of its residents believed Edwards was never hung, but instead was set free. C. N. Noteware said: "A committee took Edwards to Honey Lake for execution — but there was good reason to believe that he was never executed but that he was allowed to escape — an effigy being hanged in his stead." Henry Van Sickle reported on Walter Cosser, one of those who was assigned to view the hanging: "He says that all who went from this valley were barred from any participation in the alleged hanging of the aforesaid Bill Edwards, and that he did not believe the said (E) was ever hung by said mob....the whole affair has a suspicious odor, when we consider the haste with which Lucky Bill was hung against whom there was no positive evidence."

Although the Honey Lakers said no Carson Valley men rode with them and Cosser says Carson Valley men were barred from participation, on June 29th Samuel Swanger, Major Ormsby's clerk and real estate partner, came into Genoa with a remarkable story. He claimed that not only had he attended the hanging, but that a deposition had been taken and Edwards had changed his trial testimony. On July 3rd a letter from a man signing himself 'Quiz' was printed in the Placerville *Mountain Democrat* relaying Swanger's

Fates of the Principals   109

information: "Swanger returned from Honey Lake Valley last evening and informed me that Edwards was hang Wednesday, June 23d, 1858, between 6 and 7 o'clock P.M. Before he was hung he made a full confession and the following statement, under oath:

> Honey Lake Valley, June 23d, 1858.
> Wm. W. Edwards sworn, deposes and says: That Wm. Thorington first proposed to me the murder of Gordier when he was in Honey Lake. His proposition was to entice Gordier to Carson Valley and then murder him; when he, Thorington was to buy the Gordier stock, much below its value, as his share of the robbery.
> Myself and John Mullen were the only persons actually engaged in committing the murder of Gordier. Thorington said he could very easily conceal the murder by the evidence he would be able to produce.
> When I first went to Carson Valley, after the murder, I told Thorington we had committed it. — There was no other person but myself and Mullen went to Carson Valley. <u>The story about the man going with us, was mere fabrication.</u>
> If Snow knew anything about the murder, <u>I never told him;</u> but Mullen told me he could make him <u>do anything</u>. Snow I understood either from him or Mullen, had formerly shot a man.
> Mullen admitted to me that he had killed a Spaniard for money near Marysville, (Cal).
> I am the man who killed Snelling in Merced County, Cal., but did it in self-defense. This, the murder of Gordier, is the only crime of which I am guilty.
> This, the foregoing statement, is certified to, to the citizens of this Valley, by Messrs. Chas. C. Walden, L. N. Breed, O. Streshly, and Z. N. Spaulding, and also sworn to before a Justice of the Peace, Mr. Jno. H. Neal, of Plumas county. (I presume he is a J. P. of that county,) by the same gentlemen as being true and correct.

Although this story was picked up and printed in other newspapers, from all available evidence it must be concluded that it is a complete falsification. If true the story would have reversed the trial testimony and neatly tied up all loose ends. It said all that the Honey Lakers and Thorington's Carson Valley enemies hoped would come out at the trial: ie. Thorington first proposed the murder, he was told of it immediately upon Edwards arrival in Carson Valley and Snow had formerly killed a man (which would have helped excuse Snow's hanging). In one statement all the vigilantes' actions would have been justified. Edwards had even been sworn and deposed.

110   The Hanging of Lucky Bill

But, Swanger's statement was never corroborated. Breed and Walden, along with several others who had taken part in the vigilante action, left immediately for Canada. Neither Spaulding nor Neale, who remained at Honey Lake, ever acknowledged the statement. Similarly, neither Angel, Fairfield, Fariss and Smith nor any other historian reports that Edwards changed his testimony of the trial. Honey Laker Fred Hines rode with Edwards all the way back from Carson Valley and does not mention anything about a confession, neither does Willam Dow. Orlando Streshly and R. W. Young each reported being at the hanging (Streshly says he buried Edwards: "He requested me to take his body up to My place & bury him at the side of the road, about half way between his mining claim & Richmond & I did so.") and likewise say nothing about Edwards changing his story or offering a confession. Whether the Genoans who believed Edwards was set free or the Honey Lakers who claimed to have participated in his hanging held the truth, all concur that neither Swanger nor anyone else from Carson Valley had been present. Swanger's story can only be explained as another piece of propaganda, invented to justify the actions of the vigilantes.

R. W. Young's version of Edward's hanging offers further insight into Rough Elliot's character: "Edwards pulled off a ring from his pocket and $480.00 (as I understood at the time) from his pocket. and handed them to Ruff Elliot and requested him to send them to his mother which Elliot promised to do... I have been creditably informed that Elliot never sent the things as he promised the dying man. When Edwards was hanged it affected me so much I could not look at him so I don't know if he clapped or not."

Elzyette Knott Selby described her father Elzy Knott's actions after Thorington's arrest: "You asked me what my father did when they hung Lucky Bill. Before they hung him, he was with a bunch of men who hid in the daytime up in Genoa Canyon. At night they came down to visit their families, but they always knew where each other was, and in case of trouble, had their own signals to let each other know. After they tried Lucky Bill here in Genoa and took him down to hang him, my mother was very nervous because she thought my father was going down to look on at the hanging. Just a few days after, my mother lost my sister ahead of me by premature birth. She was so frightened over father's danger, that they might hang him, it caused her to lose the baby." Elzyette's uncle said: "After Lucky Bill was killed Elzy had to hide out for

Fates of The Principals   111

several days with a bunch of other fellows." The Committee had won control of the valley.

In Placerville after Thorington's hanging the streets were astir. On June 22nd a Sacramento *Daily Union* correspondent reported from Placerville: "There is considerable excitement in our city this evening: knots of citizens are discussing the events of the last few days. Thornton was an old resident of Placerville before settling in Carson Valley."

In other places friends of Lucky Bill and those whom he had helped were outraged. Fairfield told of the woman who called "the vengence of Heaven down upon the heads of those who hanged him." He also related two incidents involving Honey Lakers that illustrate Mormon sentiment toward Thorington's killers. William Dow was in Salt Lake City the summer of 1859 and went to the ranch of a man named Coon. "Coon told him what happened to Lucky Bill and asked Dow where he was from, and when told that he was from Honey Lake valley Coon said he must have known something about it at the time. Dow told him he heard about it. The other man looked at him very sharply and asked him if he was sure that he was not one of the crowd that did the hanging. Dow said again that he heard about it, but was very busy just then. Dow was satisfied that if the Mormons had known that he was one of the Honey Lake party, they would have killed him before he got away from there." Fairfield continued, saying: "The same year Hines had a trading post on the Humboldt River. One day a crowd of Mormons came along and stopped at his place a while. They cursed and abused the Honey Lakers for the part they took in the hanging of Lucky Bill, but Hines said it was too big a crowd for him and he kept still."

With Lucky Bill's death, Jerome and his mother took control of all Thorington property. In July they sold The White House Hotel to D. E. Gilbert, beginning a process of gradually selling off their holdings. Within a few years Jerome, still in his early twenties, drank himself to death. Maria's mind then snapped. She lived in asylums until her death around the turn of the century.

Martha Lamb lived in Carson Valley several more years. In November of 1859 she sold the 320 acres claimed by George Lamb in 1854. On July 1, 1861 David Olds' wife was granted a divorce from her husband. David Olds, Lute Olds brother, was a commissioner for the newly formed Douglas County. The petition for divorce stated in part: "That being so married to the petitioner the said David Olds — at the county of Carson and the Territory of Utah, on or about the first day of February 1861 did commit adultery with one Martha Lamb. And the said David Olds at divers times since the first day of February 1861 has committed the said crime of adultery with the said Martha Lamb."

Shortly thereafter David Olds married Martha Lamb and they left the valley. In 1866 they moved to Round Valley in Inyo County, California and lived there the rest of their lives. Martha Lamb Olds died at age 83 in 1914, five years after her husband. On January 22, 1914 her front page obituary in The *Inyo Register* said: "Whatever the unknown future holds in reward for the upright, kindly and personally honored in this life must surely be hers." In a final touch of irony regarding her relationship with Lucky Bill, the obituary's last line stated that The Eastern Star, of which she was a member, was in charge of the final tributes in the Masonic cemetery.

Lute Olds lived many years in Carson Valley. Twenty-three years after his supposed banishment Myron Angel wrote: "an unsuccessful attempt was afterwards made to collect that fine; and one of the parties, at least, still lives in Carson Valley." The one referred to was Lute Olds. Fairfield's account differed from Angel's on the payment of the fines. He quoted Joseph Frey as saying that a month or two after the trial a group of men confiscated Olds' cattle and, "A cattle man named Douglas furnished the money to pay the fine and probably took the Olds cattle for security."

On December 30, 1858 the San Francisco *Herald* reported how Olds was again warned to leave the valley. On December 11, 1858 a meeting had been chaired by Major William Ormsby. John Cary was elected President and Dr. B. L. King one of the vice presidents. Their business included the rejection of the Utah Governor's appointee, John S. Child, as Probate Judge. They were, in fact, rejecting the attempt by Utah's authorities to reorganize the county. They issued a memorial calling Utah's laws repugnant, saying an attempt by Judge Child to enforce those laws would be dealt with by "The Committee." A group of ten, including Major Ormsby, Swanger, Theodore Winters, D. H. Barber, Walter Cosser, Sides and Abernathy was formed to take the county records from The Recorder, Stephan A. Kinsey. Kinsey, getting word of their action, sent the records to Governor Cummings in Utah. The Committee's last item of business in December was to acknowledge the actions taken in June at Clear Creek Ranch and issue their threat to Olds: "The following resolutions in reference to the action

Fates of The Principals   113

of the Vigilance Committee, were also adopted:
"Resolved, That the Sheriff is hereby directed to exercise strict vigilance with regard to the deportment of L Olds; and at the expiration of the time allowed for his stay, in case he does not conform to the spirit of resolution No.1, then to summon to his assistance such men as he may deem necessary, and arrest his person and proceed to award to him the verdict rendered by the Jury, at Clear Creek Ranch, the 16th day of June, 1858."

Several things would intervene, allowing Olds to retain his Carson Valley liberty (and,in fact,his life — the sentence having been banishment under penalty of death). In Genoa on December 23, 1858 a group met to form The Law and Order Party. Comprised in part of anti-vigilantes, they called The Committee 'The Junta', and vowed that they, themselves, would obey the laws of Utah until they might form a new territory of their own.

There also were problems within The Committee, itself. A month earlier one of the vigilantes own number, a man named Alexander Chauvan was reported to have slain "a mere boy" named Fredrick Dixon over a game of cards. On November 22nd the San Francisco *Herald* reported: "A few words passed between them of trifling moment, which were not expected to lead to the slightest difficulty between the parties. The players got up from the table, and Dixon stepped outside of the house with his back to the door. While standing in this position, Chauvan drew his revolver, (navy size), standing inside, took deliberate aim at D., and fired, the ball just passing under the right ear and slightly grazing his neck. Dixon turned and saw Chauvan in the act of taking sight. He started to run, partially turning around as he was running, at the same time addressing C., and piteously begging him not to shoot. The assassin stepped to the door, took a dead rest against the frame and fired, shooting Dixon through the back. Chauvan was arrested, taken to Genoa and allowed to go at large....He was an active member of the Vigilance Committee of Carson Valley, which may account for his release. A foul murder has been committed, and the murderer has been allowed to go free, through the partiality or carelessness of the officers having him in charge."

On June 1, 1859 Tennessee included an attack on the vigilantes in his correspondence to the *Herald*: "It is a curious fact that of three homicides committed in this vicinity during the past eight months, the perpetrators of which have been known, 2 of the guilty were active members of the Vigilance Committee, and the 3rd, at his trial, was saved by the influence of that patriotic association. I mention this fact in corroboration of all past history that those who set themselves up for reformers of public evils are not always the very 'purest and best;' in 9 cases out of 10 they would be more profitably employed in plucking motes out of their own eyes, at home."

Further, The Committee's efforts at curbing the outlaw population appeared to have been far from successful. On June 29 the *Herald* printed another communique from Tennessee: "Numerous thieves and murderers run loose here and we have no tribunal before which their guilt can be proven."

Finally, Governor Cummings appointed a new judge, John Cradlebaugh. In September of 1859 Cradlebaugh arrived and took charge, appointing strong men as Grand Jury Foreman and Prosecuting Attorney. He urged indictments against all manner of criminals including, "parties alleged to have participated in the irregular judicial proceedings and executions that had occurred." Although indictments were not brought, the Judge's forthright actions were a sobering agent that countered vigilante actions.

In the spring of 1860 there would be war with the Paiute Indians. News of ore astonishingly rich in gold and silver was already causing a mad rush to the mines above Gold Canyon. The valley's bitter factionizing dissipated as many of the key players turned their attention from Carson Valley.

Elzy Knott's wife Mary lost a child shortly after Lucky Bill's hanging. In March of 1859 she was again pregnant. Her child would be born fatherless. Elzy had won a bridle playing cards against a nineteen year old Mormon, John Herring. Herring took the bridle from one of Elzy's employees. Elzy went to Herring's house to get it. Herring's mother warned Elzy not to try to take the bridle, that her son was in his room, armed. As Elzy knocked and entered Herring fired, shooting Elzy through the head. Tried before The People's Court, comprised of members of The Committee, the boy was acquitted on the grounds that he was in his home and Elzy had no right to enter. Speculation was rife among Genoa's citizenry that the boy had been set free because his father was a vigilante supporter while Elzy, Lucky Bill's good friend, had been an adamant anti-vigilante.

Lucky Bill's other close friend, Uncle Billy Rogers, abandoned the valley shortly after the hanging. Moving farther from the developing civilization, he became the first settler of Ruby Valley in Nevada's Ruby Mountains. There, acting as a sub-agent for Indian affairs, he selected land for the Shoshone Indian reservation. He also started his own farm, demonstrating that the desert

Fates of The Principals 115

land could be productive. His name was raised occasionly, as in 1862 when Charles Stebbins, formerly of Carson Valley, "in company with the famous pioneer and frontiersman William H. Rogers" packed into the Rubys to find a mystic mountain lake, dreaded by the Indians. But, as far as Carson Valley residents were concerned Uncle Billy had crossed over from citizen to legend.

It had been Rough Elliot, erstwhile friend of Edwards and Mullen, who through his detective work and testimony provided the pretext for Lucky Bill's execution. The rest of his life would follow its already established pattern, crossing and recrossing the line between law and the unlawful. His work with Carson Valley's committee for vigilance led to later involvement helping organize vigilantes in Reno. But, his violent ways would catch up with him. He spent his last years in prison in Inyo County, convicted of murder.

Richard Sides, with a partner named Jacob Rose, had taken possession of Orson Hyde's sawmill in Washoe Valley, after the Mormon elder was recalled to Salt Lake City. Hyde claimed the mill had never been paid for and demanded payment of $20,000. Sides and Rose refused, prompting the issuance, in 1862, of Orson Hyde's curse. The curse read in part: "But if you shall think best to repudiate our demand or any part of it, all right. We shall not make it up again in this world in any shape of any of you; but the said R. D. Sides and Jacob Rose shall be living and dying advertisements of God's displeasure, in their persons, in their families, in their substances; and this demand of ours, remaining uncancelled, shall be to the people of Carson and Washoe Valleys as was the ark of God among the phillistines. (See 1st Sam. fifth chapter). You shall be visited of the Lord of Hosts with thunder and with earthquakes and with floods, with pestilence and with famine until your names are not known amongst men..."

Robert Lewers, in Sam Davis' *History of Nevada*, discussed an occurrence that ensued some years after the curse: "And it is a curious instance of the accidental fulfilment of a portion of the curse, that in 1880, a flood, caused by the breaking of a mountain dam, did wash out of existence the very site of the old mill, the town below it, and covered the ranch that once belonged to Sides with such quantities of sand that it was rendered practically worthless." Another affliction struck Sides with more immediacy. This had to do with a mining claim. It was filed by Sides, Abernathy, Baldwin and a man named Belcher. They took possession of something less than 500 feet of land at Virginia City between The Ophir mine and The Gould and Curry. Finding little there the claim was given up in 1867 to the Bank Ring, as were two other small adjacent claims. Ownership then fell to four gentlemen named Fair, Mackay, Flood and O'Brian. When the big bonanaza was struck soon thereafter all previous owners discovered, too late, that under that land lay the heart of The Comstock Lode. They had let slip away the richest mine in the world.

As for Major Ormsby, his lot seems a fitting conclusion to this story. For two years after Lucky Bill's hanging he was the country's leading citizen. He moved from Genoa to Carson City. Besides his pack train business he was earning a small fortune selling general merchandise and renting rooms to miners. He also chaired most important meetings in the territory.

As more and more gold seekers flooded the territory relations between whites and Indians worsened. In April 1860 Bannocks joined the Paiutes for meetings at Pyramid Lake, north of Washoe Valley. At the beginning of May, Indians found two Paiute girls whom they had believed were lost, tied in the basement of Williams Station east of Virginia City. The Indians killed the white kidnappers and burned the station to the ground.

Word of the Indian "massacre" quickly spread. Whites demanded retribution. One of those who organized the whites was Major Ormsby. Ferol Egan wrote: "In Eagle Valley the guiding hand was none other than Major William Ormsby, who truly had been one of Walker's filibusters'. A man of excitable nature, a man quick to make a judgement, Major Ormsby was Carson City's man for a bad season. His own personality convinced others who should have known better that the time had come to teach the Indians a lesson." Albert Adams Knott said: "When Major Ormsby got all excited and asked everyone to go to war against the Indians, he came on down to Genoa and got them all stirred up to go get their muskets."

On May 10, 1860 more than one hundred volunteers formed into a hasty but eager army and started out to avenge the "massacre victims."

Major Ormsby assumed a kind of leadership over the undisciplined band, issuing directives and detailing groups as scouts and a rear guard. The Indians were confronted near Pyramid Lake. They awaited the whites on a hilltop across a meadow. They were led by the Paiute war chief, Ormsby's old friend, Numaga.

The whites fired. The Indians dismounted from their horses, firing back. The army's eagerness was quelled as a real battle began. "Major Ormsby sat stiffly in his saddle, glanced at the confused army, and shouted the command to charge. Then he spurred his tired horse and started up the slope. No more than thirty or forty men followed him..."

It was arduous work for horses, already tired from a long morning's ride, to gain the hill. When they did, the Indians had disappeared. From behind sagebrush and rocks, warriors stepped out firing volleys at the encircled whites. Ormsby called for his men to retreat. Their horses began stumbling back down the hill. The cottonwoods and brush around the meadow now came alive with Indian fire. The battle became a rout.

Ormsby was wounded in the arm and cheek, from which he had to pull an arrow. The wounds would be fatal. Tennessee reported: "[Major Ormsby] turned to Captain R. G. Watkins, and remarking that he had received a mortal wound, ordered him at all hazards to gain the pass and protect the flying troops....He last heard Ormsby imploring his men for God's sake to rally around him and not let his body fall into the hands of the savages; but 'twas in vain, the first law in nature was obeyed, and Major Ormsby fell from his horse... That he fought bravely on this occasion is admitted by all. He was well known in California and elsewhere for good or evil. He was my enemy, but he has fallen in defending his country against a savage unrelenting foe, and 'the grave shall extinguish every resentment.'"

118 The Hanging of Lucky Bill

NOTES

Extracts

10 *In the year:* Thomas Wren, A History of the State of Nevada: Its Resources and People (New York, Lewis Publishing Company, 1904) p. 36.

10 *Lucky Bill:* Quoted from the Sacramento *Daily Union,* June 19, 1857.

10 *The country:* Myron Angel, History of Nevada (Oakland, Thompson and West, 1881) p. 49.

10 *Many stories:* Henry Van Sickle, Nevada Historical Society Papers 1913-1916 (Carson City, State Printing Office, 1917) p. 192.

10 *By sharp:* J. Wells Kelly, First Directory of Nevada Territory (San Francisco, 1862), p. 23.

10 *To me:* Letter from D. R. Hawkins to A. M. Fairfield, March 12, 1912. Ms. California Room, California State Library, Sacramento.

11 *Noticed along:* Captain J. H. Simpson, Report of Explorations Across the Great Basin of the Territory of Utah (Washington D.C., Government Printing Office, 1876) p.92.

11 *The writer:* A. M. Fairfield, A Pioneer History of Lassen County, California, (San Francisco, H. S. Crocker Co., 1916) pp. 130-131.

11 *Now whether:* Harry Hawkins, ed. Mary Ellen Glass Douglas - Alpine History (Reno, University of Nevada, 1967) p. 30.

Chapter One

17 "Someone said": Archer Butler Hulbert, Forty Niners, (Las Vegas, Nevada Publications, 1986), p. 214.

18 "All kinds of": John Wood, diary quoted in "Motorland," April 1929, p. 15.

Notes 119

18 "A man owning": Henry Van Sickle, Nevada Historical Society Papers 1913-1916, p. 192.

19 "We had to": J. M. Hixon, diary quoted in "Alpine Heritage" (South Lake Tahoe, Anchor Printing, 1964) p. 19.

20 "but the most": Hulbert, Forty Niners, p. 260.

20 "His brilliant": George and Bliss Hinkle, Sierra-Nevada Lakes, (Indianapolis and New York, The Bobbs-Merrill Company, 1949) p. 142.

20 "Here, gentlemen": Quoted in David Thompson, Nevada: A History of Changes, (Reno, The Grace Dangberg Foundation, 1986) p.202.

21 "In form": Angel, History of Nevada, p. 49.

21 "In relation": Van Sickle, Nevada Historical Society Papers 1913-1916, p. 192.

21 "(Lucky Bill) was": A. H. Hawley, Nevada Historical Society Papers 1913-1916, p. 176.

21 "due to": Angel, History of Nevada, p. 49.

21 "strikingly beautiful": Nancy Miluck, "Nevada Highways & Parks," Winter Issue, 1972, p. 30.

21 "a favorite": Ibid.

21 "never worked": Emanuel Penrod, Nevada Historical Society Quarterly I volume 2. 1957, p. 62.

22 "...he was": Angel, History of Nevada, p. 36.

22 "He [Lucky Bill]": H. Hamlin, Knott Reminiscences, Early History of the 1850's (Placerville, The Pioneer Press, 1947) p. 11.

22 "In 1853": Grace Dangberg, CARSON VALLEY, Historical Sketches Of Nevada's First Settlement (Reno, The Carson

120   The Hanging of Lucky Bill

Valley Historical Society, 1972) p. 127.

22   "if they had": Honorable Thomas Wren, <u>A History of The State of Nevada, Its Resources and People</u> (New York, Lewis Publishing Company, 1904) p. 36.

23   "except two": Ibid., p. 36.

Chapter Two

24   "I was": California Senate Journal, 4 Sess. App. Doc 3, Taken from Samuel R. Davis, <u>History of Nevada</u> (Reno, The Elms Publishing Company, 1913) p. 199.

25   "when he shall": Davis, <u>History of Nevada</u>, p. 190.

26   "borrow no": Angel, <u>History of Nevada</u>, p. 50.

26   "neither an": Ibid.

26   "lite out": Ibid.

26   "Numerous incidents": Ibid., p. 51.

26   "Hundreds of": Wren, <u>A History of the State of Nevada</u>, p. 36.

26   "to Mr. William": <u>Records of Carson City, Utah and Nevada Territories 1855-61</u> (Carson City, 1861) pp. 76-77.

27   "...another man": Sarah Winnemucca Hopkins, <u>Life Among The Piutes, Their Wrongs and Claims</u>, (New York, G. P. Putnam's Sons, 1883) p. 58.

28   "Information coming": Arnold R. Trimmer, unpublished manuscript, 1969, The Van Sickle Collection, Douglas County Library.

28   "The Kingdom": Juanita Brooks, <u>Nevada Historical Society Quarterly Volume VIII Number 1</u>, Spring 1965, p. 16.

29   "Learning last": Ibid., pp. 16-17.

Notes 121

30 "...in honor": Ibid.

30 " sole and": Angel, <u>History of Nevada</u>, pp. 38-39.

Chapter Three

32 "They were": Hamlin, <u>Knott Reminiscences</u>, p. 15.

32 "In consequence": <u>Record of Probate Court of Carson County, Utah Territory October 2, 1855 to July 30, 1861.</u> Complaint filed May 22, 1856, pp. 15-16, 17-21.

33 "he 'demoralized'": H. Hamlin, <u>Knott Reminiscences</u>, p. 20.

34 "in almost": Angel, <u>History of Nevada</u>, p. 40.

35 "looked as": Ibid., P. 45.

35 "curious": Ibid., p. 145.

35 "the country": Bil Gilbert, <u>Westering Man</u> (University of Oaklahoma Press, Norman, 1985) p. 133.

35 "howling and": Ibid.

35 "the pleasure": Ibid., p. 146.

35 "Moreover, a": James F. Downs, <u>The Two Worlds of TheWasho</u>, (New York, Holt, Rinehart & Winston, 1966) p. 177

36 "mushege": Ibid., p. 146.

36 "The treaty": David Thompson, <u>Nevada Events 1776-1985,</u> (Reno, The Grace Dangberg Foundation, 1987) p. 8.

36 "there were": Angel, <u>History of Nevada</u>, p. 147.

37 "inspiring and": Ibid., p. 50.

37 "How the": Dangberg, <u>Carson Valley</u>, p. 8.

38 "Decidedly, no": Letter from D. R. Hawkins to A. M. Fairfield, March 10, 1912. The California Room, California State Library, Sacramento.

38 "The Honey": Hinkle, Sierra Nevada Lakes, p. 115.

39 "Though the": Fairfield, A Pioneer History of Lassen County, California, p. 120.

Chapter Four

42 "had been": Hawkins, Letter of March 10, 1912.

42 "Walker Filibusterer": H. Hamlin, Knott Reminiscences, p. 12.

42 "Very little": Ibid.

42 "He (Ormsby)": Egan, Sand In A Whirlwind, The Paiute Indian War of 1860, p. 27.

42 "a man of": Ibid., p. 114.

42 "blunt," "excited": Ibid., p. 31-32.

45 "I know": Hopkins, Life Among The Paiutes: Their Wrongs And Claims, p.61.

46 "Some said": Ibid.

46 "Just then": Ibid., p. 62.

46 "It seemed": Katherine Gehn, Sarah Winnemucca, Most Extraordinary Woman of the Paiute Nation, (Phoenix, O'Sullivan, Woodside & Co., 1975) p. 39.

Chapter Five

47 "...while here": Van Sickle, Nevada Historical Society 1913-1916, p. 190.

48 "...Said county": Angel, History of Nevada, p. 42.

Notes

49 "an armed": Wren, <u>A History of The State of Nevada, Its Resources and People</u>, p. 31.

50 "The property": Angel, <u>History of Nevada</u>, p. 42.

Chapter Six

51 "Well lots": Hawkins, <u>Douglas - Alpine History</u>, p. 29.

51 "hard characters": Fairfield, <u>A Pioneer History of Lassen County, California</u>, pp. 130-131.

51 "for the purpose": Angel, <u>History of Nevada</u>, pp. 42-43.

52 "without any": Ibid., pp. 43-44.

52 "great harmony": Ibid., p. 45.

Chapter Seven

55 "Both sides": Hamlin, <u>Knott Reminiscences</u>, p. 11.

56 "What do": Elzyette Knott Selby as quoted by Hamlin, <u>Knott Reminiscences</u>, p. 18.

56 "came to": Ibid., p. 15.

56 "...Elzy said": Dangberg, <u>Carson Valley</u>, p. 53.

56 "After Lucky": Albert Adams Knott, <u>Knott Reminiscences</u> p. 15.

56 "Down came": Dangberg, <u>Carson Valley</u>, p. 53.

57 "Lute Olds": Selby, <u>Knott Reminiscences</u>, p. 19.

58 "Theodore Hawkins": Hamlin, <u>Knott Reminiscences</u>, p. 16.

58 "gentlemanly, kind": Hawkins, Letters of March 10 and March 12, 1912.

58 "a man": Dangberg, <u>Carson Valley</u>, pp. 41-43.

124   The Hanging of Lucky Bill

58   "a better": Van Sickle, <u>Nevada Historical Society Papers 1913-1916</u>, pp. 191-192.

58   "Sam rode": Dangberg, <u>Carson Valley</u>, p. 141.

59   "'Mannie' or": Davis, <u>The History of Nevada</u>, p. 998.

59   "He (Comstock)": Dan DeQuille, <u>The Big Bonanza</u>, (Hartford, American Publishing Company, 1876) pp. 26-27.

59   "But there": Penrod, <u>Nevada Historical Society Quarterly I Volume 2</u>, p. 64.

59   "...but was": Letter from Emanual Penrod to A. M. Fairfield, July 22, 1912.

60   "The next": Hopkins, <u>Life Among The Paiutes: Their Wrongs and Claims</u>, p. 58.

60   "...but I have": David Thompson, <u>Tennessee's Letters: From Carson Valley 1857-1860</u>, (Reno, The Grace Dangberg Foundation, 1983) p. 26.

60   "The people": Angel, <u>History of Nevada</u>, p. 49.

60   "well armed": Hamlin, <u>Knott Reminiscences</u>, p. 20.

61   "...rather than": Dangberg, <u>Carson Valley</u>, p. ix.

61   "the excitement": Angel, <u>History of Nevada</u>, p. 552.

61   "justice for": Egan, <u>Sand In A Whirlwind: The Paiute Indian War of 1860</u>, p. 23.

62   "two of": Hinkle, <u>Sierra Nevada Lakes</u>, pp. 139 and 161.

62   "Jack Demming": Egan, <u>Sand In A Whirlwind: The Paiute Indian War of 1860</u>, p. 55.

62   "Some of": Ibid, pp. 59-60.

62 "undoubted veracity": Fairfield, A Pioneer History of Lassen County, California, p. 132.

62 "Merrill: Mr.": Letter from N. E. Spoon to A. M. Fairfield, January 14, 1914.

63 "The testimony": Letter from Chauncey N. Noteware to A. M. Fairfield, n.d.

Chapter Eight

65 "At a later": D. R. Hawkins letter to Fairfield, March 12, 1912.

66 "we (Jack and myself)": Quoted in the Sacramento Daily Union, June 25, 1858. (This, and all quotes from the Union on this date come from C.N. Noteware's transcription of Lucky Bill's trial).

66 "...being at": Ibid.

66 "What luck": Ibid.

67 "for the purpose": Effie Mona Mack, Nevada: A History of the State from the Earliest Times Through the Civil War, (Glendale, The Arthur H. Clark Co., 1936) p. 177.

67 "There were": Hamlin, Knott Reminiscences, p. 20.

68 "You and I": Fairfield, A Pioneer History of Lassen County, California, p. 185.

69 "He (Eliot)": Ibid., p. 123.

69 "beat him": Ibid., p. 93.

69 "I'll get": Ibid.

69 "Probably saving": Ibid.

69 "The whites": Ibid., p. 114.

69 "The two": Ibid., p. 118.

126 The Hanging of Lucky Bill

70 "Mullen had": Ibid., p. 123.

70 "Edwards then": Noteware letter to Fairfield, n.d.

70 "...they struck": Fairfield, A Pioneer History of Lassen County, California, p. 124.

Chapter Nine

89 "The Goose Lake": Fairfield, A Pioneer History of Lassen County, California, p. 125.

89 "...she dreamed": Ibid., p. 127.

90 "There was": Letter from Orlando Streshley to A. M. Fairfield, 1913. The California Room, California State Library, Sacramento.

90 "He [Snow]": Fairfield, A Pioneer History of Lassen County, California, p. 128.

90 "John Neale": Ibid., p. 129.

91 "some considered": Letter from R. W. Young to A. M. Fairfield, August 24, 1910. The California Room, California State Library, Sacramento.

91 "...suspicion then": Noteware, Letter to Fairfield, n.d.

91 "get out": Quoted in the Sacramento Daily Union, June 25, 1858.

92 "Thorington has": Ibid.

92 "I got": Ibid.

92 "making himself": Ibid.

92 "run off": Ibid.

92 "McBride told": Ibid.

93 "Thorington told": Ibid.

Notes 127

93 "I tried": Ibid.

93 "there was": Ibid.

93 "Thorington then": Ibid.

Chapter Ten

95 "There is": Fairfield, <u>A Pioneer History of Lassen County, California</u>, p. 133.

95 "got sick": Ibid., p. 134.

96 "He (Tutt)": Ibid., p. 127.

96 "In Washoe": Ibid., p. 135.

96 "Major Ormsby": Ibid.

96 "but": Young, Letter to Fairfield, August 24, 1910.

97 "At the age": D. R. Hawkins letter to Fairfield, March 12, 1912.

97 "that afternoon": Fairfield, <u>A Pioneer History of Lassen County, California</u>, p. 137.

99 "very few": Letter from D. H. Holdridge to A. M. Fairfield, April 1, 1916. Ms. California Room, California State Library, Sacramento.

99 "The majority": Fariss and Smith, <u>Illustrated History of Plumas, Lassen and Sierra Counties, California</u>, (San Francisco, 1882) p. 388.

100 "They told": Young, Letter to Fairfield, August 24, 1910.

100 "It has been": Fairfield, <u>A Pioneer History of Lassen County, California</u>, p. 137.

100 "...the first": Ibid., p. 138.

The Hanging of Lucky Bill

101 "Joseph Frey": Ibid., pp. 138-139.

101 "I saw": Hawkins, Letter to Fairfield, March 12, 1912.

101 "A jury": Noteware, Letter to Fairfield, n.d.

101 "They were": Hawkins, Letter to Fairfield, March 12, 1912.

100 "They were": Noteware, Letter to Fairfield, n.d.

101 "The judges": Fariss and Smith, Illustrated History of Lassen, Plumas and Sierra Counties, California, p.388.

102 "he said": Quoted in the Sacramento Daily Union, June 25, 1858.

102 "The evidence": Angel, History of Nevada, pp. 50-51.

103 "Thorington had": Quoted from the Sacramento Daily Union, June 25, 1858.

103 "At the time": Ibid.

103 "Thorington told": Ibid.

103 "L. M. Breed, sworn": Ibid.

104 "get money": Ibid.

104 "Dow says:" Fairfield, A Pioneer History of Lassen County, California, p. 141.

Chapter Eleven

105 "The actions": Penrod, Nevada Historical Society Quarterly I Volume 2, pp. 62-64.

105 "am familiar": Penrod, Letter to Fairfield, July 22, 1912.

106 "The jury": Noteware, Letter to Fairfield, n.d.

107 "Young says": Fairfield, A Pioneer History of Lassen County, California, p. 141.

Notes 129

107 "A cool": Ibid.

107 "when the": Young, Letter to Fairfield, August 24, 1910.

107 "...they drew": Hamlin, Knott Reminiscences, p. 20.

107 "The Committee": Dangberg, Carson Valley, p. 29.

Chapter Twelve

108 "...(Anti vigilantes)": Hamlin, Knott Reminiscences, p. 16.

108 "He (Edwards)": Fairfield, A Pioneer History of Lassen County, California, p. 142.

108 "He says": Van Sickle, Nevada Historical Society Papers 1913-1916, p. 191.

110 "He requested": Streshly, Letter to Fairfield, 1913.

110 "Edwards pulled": Young, Letter to Fairfield, August 24, 1910.

110 "You asked": Hamlin, Knott Reminiscences, p. 20.

110 "After Lucky Bill": Ibid.. p. 15.

111 "the vengence": Fairfield, A Pioneer History of Lassen County, California, p. 131.

111 "Coon told": Ibid., pp. 143-144.

111 "That being": Nevada State Library and Archives Territorial Divorce Records, July 4, 1861.

112 "an unsuccessful": Angel, History of Nevada, p. 51.

112 "a cattle man": Fairfield, A Pioneer History of Lassen County, California, p. 144.

115 "in company": Angel, History of Nevada, p. 31.

130   The Hanging of Lucky Bill

115 "But if": Ibid., p. 41.

115 "And it is": Davis, <u>The History of Nevada</u>, p. 232.

116 "In Eagle Valley": Egan, <u>Sand In A Whirlwind: The Paiute Indian War of 1860</u>, p. 114.

116 "When Major Ormsby": Hamlin, <u>Knott Reminiscences</u>, p. 14.

116 "Major Ormsby": Egan, <u>Sand In A Whirlwind: The Paiute Indian War of 1860</u>, p. 137.

117 "[Major Ormsby]":Thompson,<u>The Tennessee Letters:From Carson Valley 1857-1860</u>, pp. 138-139.

BIBLIOGRAPHY

Alpine Heritage. The Centennial Book Committee. South Lake Tahoe: Anchor Printing, 1964.

Angel, Myron T., ed. History of Nevada. Oakland: Thompson & West, 1881.

Ashbaugh, Don. Nevada's Turbulent Yesterday ...a Study in Ghost Towns. Las Vegas: Westernlore Press, 1963.

Brooks, Juanita. "The Mormons in Carson County, Utah Territory," Nevada Historical Society Quarterly Volume VIII Number 1. Spring, 1955.

Cradlebaugh, William M. "Nevada Biography," Nevada Historical Society Papers 1913-1916.

Dangberg, Grace. Carson Valley: Historical Sketches of Nevada's First Settlement. Reno: The Carson Valley Historical Society, 1972.

_____., ed. An Inventory and Index to The Recordsof Carson County, Utah and Nevada Territories 1855-1861. Reno, 1984.

Davis, Samuel R., ed. The History of Nevada. Reno: The Elms Publishing Co., 1913.

Downs, James F. The Two Worlds of the Washo. New York: Holt, Rinehart & Winston, 1966.

De Quille, Dan. The Big Bonanza. Hartford: American Publishing Company, 1876. (Reprinted Alfred A. Knopf, 1947).

Egan, Ferol. Sand In A Whirlwind: The Paiute Indian War of 1860. New York: Doubleday & Co., 1972.

Fairfield, Asa Merrill. A Pioneer History of Lassen County, California. San Francisco: H.S. Crocker Co., 1916.

_____. Letter to D.R. Hawkins. Susanville, California. March 6, 1912. Ms. California Room, California State Library, Sacramento.

First Records of Carson Valley 1851-1855. Genoa, 1855. Nevada State Archives.

Gehn, Katherine. Sarah Winnemucca: Most Extraordinary Woman of The Paiute Nation. Phoenix: O'Sullivan, Woodside & Co., 1975.

Gilbert, Bil, Westering Man. Norman: University of Oklahoma

Press, 1985.

Hamlin, H.H., ed. Thomas Knott Reminiscences. Placerville: The Pioneer Press, 1947.

Hawkins, D.R. Letter to A.M. Fairfield. Genoa, Nevada. March 10, 1912. Ms. California Room, California State Library, Saramento.

_____. Letter to A.M. Fairfield. Genoa, Nevada. March 12, 1912. Ms. California Room, California State Library, Sacramento.

Hawkins, Harry. Douglas-Alpine History. Ed., Mary Ellen Glass. Oral History Program. University of Nevada. Reno: University of Nevada Library, 1966.

Hawley, A.H. "Lake Tahoe," Nevada Historical Society 1913-1916.

Hinkle, George and Bliss. Sierra Nevada Lakes. Indianapolis and New York: The Bobbs-Merrill Co., 1949.

Holdridge, D.H. Letter to A.M. Fairfield. San Francisco, California. April 1, 1916. Ms. California Room, California State Library, Sacramento.

Hopkins, Sarah Winnemucca. Life Among The Paiutes: Their Wrongs and Claims. Ed., Mrs Horace Mann. New York: G.P. Putnam's Sons, 1883.

Hulbert, Archer Butler. Forty Niners. Las Vegas: Nevada Publications, 1986.

Illustrated History of Plumas, Lassen and Sierra Counties, California. San Francisco: Fariss and Smith, 1882.

Jones, D.R. Letter to Robert Trimmer. Gardenerville, Nevada. April 25, 1914. Ms. The Van Sickle Collection, Douglas County Library.

Kelly, J. Wells. First Directory of Nevada Territory. San Francisco, 1862. Ms. The California Room, California State Library, Sacramento.

Lord, Eliot. Comstock Mining and Miners. Washington D.C.: Government Printing Office, 1883.

Mack, Effie Mona. Nevada: A History of the State from the Earliest Times Through the Civil War. Glendale: The Arthur H. Clark Co., 1936.

_____. "Nevada's First Newspapers," Nevada Magazine. September, 1945.

Miluck, Nancy C., ed. The Genoa-Carson Valley Book: Where Nevada Began Vol. III. Genoa, Nevada. 1981.

_____. "How Lucky Bill's Luck Ran Out In Old Genoa," Nevada Highways & Parks. Winter Issue, 1972.

Bibliography

<u>Nevada State Library and Archives Territorial Divorce Records</u>. Carson City, 1861. Nevada State Archives.

Noteware, Chauncey N. Letter to A.M. Fairfield. Carson City, Nevada. nd. Ms. California Room, California State Library, Sacramento.

Penrod, Emanual. "A Life of Fifty Years in Nevada," <u>Nevada Historical Society Quarterly I Volume 2</u>. 1957.

_____. Letter to A.M. Fairfield. Vallejo, California. July 22, 1912. Ms. California Room, California State Library, Sacramento.

_____. Letter to A.M. Fairfield. Vallejo, California. August 3, 1912. Ms. California Room, California State Library, Sacramento.

<u>Records of Carson City, Utah and Nevada Territories 1855-61</u>. Carson City, 1861. Ms. Nevada State Archives.

<u>Records of Probate Court of Carson County, Utah Territory October 2, 1855 to July 30, 1861</u>. Carson City, 1861. Ms. Nevada State Archives.

Reese, John. "Mormon Station," <u>Nevada Historical Society Papers 1913-1916</u>.

Simpson, J.H. <u>Report of Explorations Across The Great Basin of The Territory of Utah</u>. Washington D.C.: U.S. Government Printing Office, 1876. (Reprinted Reno: University of Nevada Press, 1983).

Spoon, N.E. (for William Dow). Letter to A.M. Fairfield. Pacific Grove, California. January 14, 1914. Ms. California Room, California State Library, Sacramento.

Streshley, Orlando. Letter to A.M. Fairfield. Susanville? 1913? Ms. California Room, California State Library, Sacramento.

Thompson, David. <u>Nevada A History of Changes</u>. Reno: The Grace Dangberg Foundation, 1986.

_____. <u>Nevada Events 1776 - 1985</u>. Reno: The Grace Dangberg Foundation, 1987.

_____., ed. <u>The Tennessee Letters: From Carson Valley 1857-1860</u>. Reno: The Grace Dangberg Foundation, 1983.

Trimmer, Arnold R. <u>Reminiscences of The Number One Ranch in Carson Valley, Nevada</u>. Oral History Program. University of Nevada. Reno: University of Nevada Library, 1982.

_____. "Lucky Bill Thorington." Genoa, Nevada 1969. Ms. The Van Sickle Collection, Douglas County Library.

Van Sickle, Henry. "Utah Desperadoes," <u>Nevada Historical Society Papers 1913-1916</u>.

Wood, John. "Along The Emigrant Trail...diary of John Wood written in 1850," Motor Land, April, 1929.

Wren, Thomas, ed. A History of the State of Nevada: Its Resources and People. New York: Lewis Publishing Co., 1904.
Wright, William (Dan DeQuille). The Big Bonanza. Introduction by Oscar Lewis. New York: Alfred A. Knopf, Inc., 1947.
Young, R.W. Letter to A. M. Fairfield. Crescent Mills, California. August 24, 1910. Ms. California Room, California State Library, Sacramento.

Newspapers

Inyo County Register. Bishop, California. January 22, 1914.
Placerville Mountain Democrat. Placerville, California. September 5, 1857, October 31, 1857, December 1857, June 26, 1858.
Sacramento Daily Bee. Sacramento, California. June 18, 1858.
Sacramento Daily Union. Sacramento, California. June 19, 1857,
San Francisco Daily Alta. San Francisco, California. June, 1858.
San Francisco Herald. San Francisco, California. January 1, 1853, August 19, 1853, January 23, 1854, September 28, 1854, July 17, 1855, May 3, 1856, May-December 1857, March-June 1858, November 1858, June 29, 1859.
The Deseret News. Provo, Utah. July-August 1857.

INDEX

Abernathy, L.B., 25, 32, 33, 53, 54, 60, 61, 67, 97, 112, 115
Alden, Mr., 99
Allen, Richard N., 44, 92, 102 . See also Tennessee.
Angel, Myron, 10, 21-23, 26, 36, 60, 61, 72, 102, 110,112
Anti-Mormons, 47, 55, 60, 65 . See also Committee,The.
Anti-vigilantes, 56, 58, 84, 101,108, 113, 114
Arnold, Henry, 95
Atchison, T.J., 102
Austin, Calvin, 57,92, 97, 102
Averill Hill, 108

Baker, Martha. See Lamb, Martha.
Baldwin, John M., 25, 32, 33, 60, 67, 97,107, 115
Bank Ring, The, 116
Bannen, 102
Bannock Indians, 116
Barber D.H., 93, 94, 106, 112
Barnard, E.L., 25, 26
Barnard, J.L., 18
Baxter, John, 95
Beasley, 66, 67
Belcher, 115
Bidwell-Bartleson Party, 35
Boarder Ruffians, 56, 57, 87
Boone, Daniel, 19
Breed, L.N., 90, 102, 103, 109,110
Brigham's Legislature, 24
Brooks, Juanita, 29
Brown, 43
Brown, Longhaired Sam, 58
Buchanan, President, 49
Buckner, 100

California, 17, 20, 22, 24-26, 29, 34, 36, 38, 41, 46, 50, 57, 64,

68, 117
Captain Jim, 45, 46
Canada, 110
Carson Canyon, 19, 22
Carson, Christopher Kit, 18, 22, 35
Carson City, 41, 56, 59, 116
Carson County, 25, 30, 38, 48-50, 60, 67, 112
Carson River, 17-19, 30, 37, 42, 58, 68
Carson Valley, 17-25, 27-30, 33, 34, 36-39, 42, 44, 48, 50-58, 61-68, 70, 71, 76, 79, 80, 90-92, 95-99, 101, 103, 104, 106-115
Carson Valley Bridge, 26, 29
Cary, Harry, 57, 61
Cary, John 25, 33, 38, 55, 57, 61, 67, 100, 101, 112
Cary, William, 48, 57
Castro, John, 32
Chalk Hill, 23
Chapman, Alec., 69, 95, 96
Chartz, 60
Chauvan, Alexander, 67, 113
Chenango County, New York, 21
Cherry, B., 66, 67, 102, 104
Child, Judge John, 60, 68, 112
Cisco, 65
City of Saints, 50
Clark, William H., 95
Clear Creek, 23, 36, 60, 75, 101
Clear Creek Ranch, 32, 41, 60, 67, 97, 101, 106, 112, 113
Cloud, 67
Colorado River, 52
Columbus, 30
Committee, The, 29, 63, 67, 68, 79, 82, 84, 87, 94, 96, 106, 107, 111-114. See also Vigilantes.
Comstock, H.T.P., 59
Comstock Lode, 59, 116
Coombs, William, 65-67, 90, 92, 100, 103. See also Edwards, William Coombs.

Coon, 111
Coper, Mr., 32
Cosser, Walter, 87, 108, 112
Cotton Hotel, 57, 58, 81, 97
Coulthurst, Mrs., 89
Cradlebaugh, Judge John, 114
Craft, Mat., 95, 96
Crandall, Jared, 50, 52, 68
Crandall Stagelines, 50, 61, 106
Crane, Judge, 43, 52
Crawford, William M., 95
Crawford Ranch, 66
Cummings, Governor, 61, 112, 114
Curry, Abraham, 41
Curtis, Dr., 51

Daggett, Dr. C.S., 27, 32, 33, 65, 94, 98
Daggett, Rollin, 20
Dangberg, Grace, 37, 57, 58, 107
Dangberg, H.F., 37, 71
Davis, John C., 95
Davis, Samuel R., 59, 115
Demming, Dexter, 62
Demming, Jack, 62
Deseret News, 48, 49
DeQuille, Dan, 59
Dixie Valley Indians, 69
Dixon, Fredrick, 113
Douglas, 112
Douglas County, 63, 111
Dow, William, 61, 62, 69, 96, 100, 101, 104, 110, 111
Downs, James F., 35
Dorn, John L., 18, 19
Drummond, C.W., 34

Eagle Ranch, 26

Eagle Valley, 18, 19, 21, 26, 27, 33, 34, 41, 52, 55,59, 60, 99, 101, 116
Eastern Star, 112
Eddy, Mr., 24
Edwards, William Coombs, 64-66, 69, 70, 87, 89-95, 97, 98, 100-105, 108-110, 115. See also Coombs, William.
Egan, Ferol, 42, 62, 116
El Dorado County, 25
Elko County, 59
Elliot, W.T.C. Rough, 65-69, 90, 92-94, 96, 97, 99-103, 105, 107, 108-110, 115
Emigrant Canyon toll road, 19, 29, 54, 56
Emigrant Trail, the, 17, 24, 56
Epstein, A.G., 95

Fain, J.C., 30
Fair, Mackay, Flood and O'Brian, 116
Fairfield, Asa Merrill, 11, 38, 39, 42, 58, 59, 62, 68-70, 73, 85, 89, 90, 95-97, 100, 101, 104, 105, 107, 108, 110-112
Fariss and Smith, 99, 101, 110
Ferry, J.H. Blackhawk, 69
Forty Mile Desert, The, 17,
France, 89
Fredrich, W. 33
Fredricksburg Ranch, the, 20, 27, 57, 75
Fremont expedition, the, 35
Frey, Joseph, 101, 112
Frey, Lawrence, 107

Gandy, Issac, 57, 97, 102
Gehn, Katherine, 46
Genoa, 18, 20, 21, 28, 30, 31, 33, 36-38, 40, 41, 44, 53, 56, 57, 65, 67, 68, 81, 91, 94-97, 101, 108, 110, 113, 114, 116
Genoa Canyon, 56, 110
Gilbert, D.E., 51-53, 102, 111
Gilbert's Saloon, 51

Gilpin, Junius Brutus, 65-67, 69, 90, 93, 100-102
Gold Canyon, 19, 22, 30, 41, 114
Goose Creek, 43, 44
Goose Creek Range, 52
Goose Lake, 69, 89
Gordier, Henry, 70, 89-91, 93, 103, 104, 106, 109
Gould and Curry Mine, 115
Gravelly Ford, 43
Gray, Orin, 52, 97, 98, 102
Great American Basin, 17, 35, 52, 60
Gullion, Jerry, 20

Haines, Mrs, 67, 97. See also Mrs. Singleton.
Hamlin, H., 22, 42, 55, 58, 67
Hardin, Mr., 43
Harris, Mary, 56
Harvey, Thomas J., 95
Haviland, Mark, 95
Hawes, 102
Hawkins, C., 77
Hawkins, D.R., 10, 37, 38, 42, 58, 65, 74, 97, 99, 101
Hawkins, Harry, 11, 51
Hawkins, John, 57, 58, 97
Hawkins, Sarah Jane, 57
Hawkins, Theodore, 58
Hawley, A.H., 21
Henderson, 95
Hepperly, G.W., 101
Herring, John, 114
Hickman, Bill, 35
Hill, Cap, (William Hill Naileigh), 95
Hines, Fred, 95, 110, 111
Hinkle, George and Bliss, 20, 62
Hixon, J.M., 19
Holbrook, Charles, 37
Holdridge, D.H., 99

Hollinhead, J., 32
Honey Lake, 38, 52, 62, 66, 68-70, 80, 86, 89, 90, 92, 94, 95, 98-101, 103, 104, 108, 110
Honey Lake Rangers, 62, 95
Honey Lakers, 39, 61, 62, 68, 69, 89, 91, 92, 95, 96, 99, 108-111
Honey Lake Valley, 61, 64-66, 68, 90-93, 95, 99, 103, 104, 109, 111
Hopkins, Sarah Winnemucca, 27, 40, 45, 46, 60
Howard, George, 36
Howard, Jack, 66
Hughes, 95
Hulbert, Archer Butler, 17, 20
Humboldt River, 17, 35, 111
Humboldt Sink, 17
Hyde, Orson, 28, 30, 32-34, 48, 49, 60, 79, 115

Illinois, 36
Inyo County, 28, 112, 115
Inyo County Register, 28, 112

Jerry, 106, 107
Johnson, Frank, 95
Johnson, Governor, 44
Johnson, Mr.
Johnston, General Sydney,
Jones, Issac N., 68

Kelly, J. Wells, 10
Kentucky, 41
King, B.L., 33, 101, 112
Kinsey Stephen A., 32, 33 57, 61, 112
Klauber Ranch, 37
Knott, Albert Adams, 32, 116
Knott, Elzy, 32, 33, 55, 56, 67, 84, 110, 114
Knott, Mary, 114. See also Harris, Mary.
Knott, Thomas, 18, 22, 26, 27, 32, 42, 55, 56, 61
Know Nothing Boys, 66

Lake Tahoe, 35
Lamb, George, 27, 111
Lamb, Martha, 27, 28, 53-55, 77, 100,107, 111, 112
Lassen, Peter, 38, 52, 61, 95
Lathrop, George, 95
Law and Order Party, 113. See also anti-vigilantes.
Lewers, Robert, 115
Loveland, Judge Chester, 48, 50
Lovell, P.H., 53
Lucky Bill. See Thorington, William R.

Mack, Effie Mona, 67
Marysville, 41, 92, 109
Masons, 64, 96, 105, 112
Mast, Ben, 37
McBride, 92, 93, 97, 102
McLaughlin, Pat, 59
McMarland, John, 43-46
McMurtry, Tom., 95, 103, 104
McVeagh, 95
Mead, A., 33
Meek, Joe, 35
Menofee, James, 66
Merced County, 64, 66, 69, 90, 92, 103, 109
Merkeley, C., 32
Meyers, William, 95
Michigan, 21, 27
Montgomery, Mr., 28
Mormon Church, 23
Mormons, 18, 28-30, 32, 33, 38, 47-51, 54, 55, 60, 65, 68-70, 105, 111, 115
Mormon Party, The, 47
Mormon Station, 18, 19, 24-26, 30. See also Genoa.
Mote, John, 95
Mott, H., 32-34, 93

Mott, J., 32-34, 93
Mountain Meadow masacre, 49, 50
Mullen, John, 69, 70, 89-92, 109, 115
Munchie, D.M., 95

Natchez, 45
Neale, John, 90, 95, 101, 109, 110
Nevada, 18, 20, 26, 36, 46, 51, 63, 96, 97
Nevada Territory, 63
Neversweats, 39, 68, 69, 94, 95, 97
Nicaragua, 42, 60
Norton, Thad., 95
Noteware, C.N. Chauncey, 62, 63, 70, 86, 91, 96, 99, 101-104, 106-108
Numaga (Young Winnemucca), 35, 45, 61, 83, 116

Ohio, 32
Old Emigrant Road, 26
Olds, David, 57, 111, 112
Olds, John, 57
Olds, Luther Lute, 33, 56-58, 81, 87, 92, 97, 98, 102, 105, 111-113
Ophir mine, 115
Oregon, 52
O'Reily, Peter, 59
Ormsby County, 46
Ormsby, Major William, 38, 40-46, 50, 52, 55, 60, 61, 65, 67, 68, 82, 83, 93, 94, 96, 98-100, 106, 108, 112, 116, 117
Ormsby, Mrs. Margaret, 40, 46
Owens, Mormon Joe, 95

Paiute Indians, 27, 34-36, 42, 44-46, 61, 65, 66, 83, 114, 116
Penrod, Emanual Manny, 21, 59, 85, 87, 101, 105
People's Court, 61
Perrin, Solomon, 33, 66, 95, 103, 104
Pierce, President, 34

Pine Nut Mountains, 17
Pine Nut Valley, 45
Pit River Indians, 69
Placerville, 19, 22, 25, 36, 42, 43, 48, 49, 51, 52, 63, 68, 98, 111
Placerville Mountain Democrat, 29, 48, 49, 53, 106-108
Placerville Tri-Weekly Register, 63
Plumas County, 109
Pony, 58
Pony Express, 58
Price, Mary Ann, 30
Pyramid Lake, 116

Quiz, 108

Ragtown, 68
Ranch Camp, 28
Reese, Colonel John, 18, 19, 21, 25-27, 29, 30, 32, 33, 47, 51, 55
Reese, Enoch, 27, 32
Reno, 115
Richmond, 110
Rocky Canyon, 19
Rocky Mountains, 35
Rogers, Colonel William (Uncle Billy), 25, 43-45, 50-55, 61, 64, 65, 67, 68, 101, 107, 114, 115
Roop, Issac, 38, 52, 61, 95
Rose, Jacob, 115
Rough and Ready, 69
Round Valley, 112
Ruby Mountains, the, 114, 115
Ruby Valley, 114

S., 10, 51
Sacramento, 19, 20, 27, 41, 44, 45, 53, 64
Sacramento Daily Bee, 99, 102
Sacramento Union, 43, 50, 63, 94, 96, 97, 99, 101, 106, 111
Salt Lake City, 19, 25, 33, 47, 48, 50, 92, 111, 115

Salt Lake County, 48
Salt Lake Territory, 24
San Francisco, 68
San Francisco Daily Alta, 64, 90, 96-98, 102
San Francisco Golden Era, 20
San Francisco Herald, 19, 22, 24, 25, 28, 29, 33, 36, 37, 42-45, 48-50, 52-54, 57, 64, 65, 67, 68, 98, 100, 112-114
San Juaquin River, 98
Sawtooth, 56
Scott, R.J., 95, 96
Selby, Elzyette Knott, 56, 57, 107, 110
Shoshone Indians, 34, 35, 43, 44, 114
Sides, Richard, 25, 32, 33, 41, 51-54, 60, 61, 67, 93, 97, 100, 101, 106, 112, 115
Sierra Nevada Mountains, 17-19, 24, 38, 52, 63, 64, 91, 101
Simpson, Captain J.H., 11
Singleton, T.J., 97, 102
Singleton Hotel, 97
Singleton, Mrs., 67
Sisco, 65
Skyhawk, W.F., 57
Smith, Ab., 66
Smith, Joseph, 23
Snelling, 64, 66, 90, 96, 98, 109
Snow, Asa, 70, 89-91, 97, 99, 109
South America, 91
Spaulding, Z.N., 109, 110
Spoon, N.E., 62
Squires, A.P., 67, 107
State Journal, 50
Statesman, 99
Stebbins, Charles, 115
Stewart, 66
Storff, Antone, 95
Streshly, Orlando, 90, 95, 109, 110
Susan River, 38, 66, 89

Index   145

Susanville, 38
Swanger, Samuel, 38, 41, 60, 108, 109, 110, 112

Tennessee, 44, 64, 65, 68, 92, 113, 114, 117. See also Richard Allen.
Thompson and West, 63, 108
Thompson, John Snowshoe, 36, 42, 48, 65, 67, 94
Thompson, Richard, 95
Thorington, Maria, 21, 27, 96, 107, 111
Thorington, William B. Lucky Bill (a.k.a. Thornton,Thorrington), 19-22, 25-27, 29, 31-33, 36-39, 41, 48, 51-76, 80-82, 84, 86, 87, 91-111, 114, 116
Thorington, William Jerome, 21, 27, 65, 92, 94, 96, 98, 100, 102, 103, 107, 111
Thorington, William R., 28
Thornton, William. See Thorington, William B.
Thissel, G. W., 20
Townsend, James, 29
Trimmer, Arnold, 28
Trumbo, J.K., 46
Tutt, U.J., 62, 95

Utah, 18, 24, 25, 30, 38, 47-49, 60, 61, 112
Utah Territory, 20, 24, 25, 30, 34-36, 38, 47, 60, 98, 112

Vallely, Peter, 92, 102
Van Sickle, Henry, 10, 18, 21, 27, 30, 33, 47, 56, 58, 59, 76, 99, 108
Vigilantes (vigilance committee), 19, 29, 38, 53, 54, 56, 58, 67, 68, 73, 100, 105, 113, 115. See also The Committee.
Virginia City, 115, 116

Wade, W.B., 38, 100
Walden, Chas. C., 109, 110
Walker, Joseph, 35
Walker, William, 42, 60, 116
Washoe Indians, 18, 23, 34, 35, 40, 42-46, 64

Order Form

Please send me _____ copy(ies) of **The Hanging of Lucky Bill**, autographed and inscribed by Michael Makley. I include $9.95 for each book and $1.75 for the shipping of the first book, .75 for each additional book.

Name_____

Address_____

City_____State_____ Zip_____

Total for books $_____

Send checks or money order to:

Eastern Sierra Press
16 Pioneer Trail
Woodfords, California 96120

Thanks for your mail order!